D1588956

30

Reading the Bible

*In the run-up
to death*

By the same author:

On Language and writing (1947)

*The Concept of the Avant Garde,
and other essays* (1973)

*The Cat Sat on the Mat:
Language and the Absurd* (2002)

In preparation:
Memoirs of a Language Freak

Reading the Bible
Bible

*In the run-up
to death*

John Weightman

Weech Publishing

2206

Weech Publishing
15 Kelross Road
London N5 2QS
gavin.weightman@btinternet.com

Published by Weech Publishing 2003

A catalogue record for this book is
available from the British Library

ISBN 0-9543296-1-9

Set in Garamond by Graham Curd

Cover illustration by Clare Beaton

Printed and bound by
Antony Rowe Ltd.
Bumper's Farm Industrial Estate.
Chippenham,
Wiltshire

To the memory of my wife and
our fifty years together: 1935-85

Epigraph

*"On croit toujours à quelque chose. Celui qui doute croit à soi qui doute.
Cette foi en soi seul sera appelée orgueil."* (Paul Valéry)

(We cannot avoid belief. He who doubts believes in himself, the doubter.
This faith in the individual self will be called pride.)

Contents

Preface

Why this title? Because, if you live long enough, there is a point in old age at which you come out, as it were, into the open, on the far side of life. Before you is *la dernière ligne droite*, the run-up to the finish. You don't know how long or how short it will be but, as the last phase of consciousness, it has its own peculiar interest.

I wish to thank my friend, Rodney Needham, for many illuminating discussions about religion and kindred matters; this is not to say that he necessarily shares my views.

I am grateful to other friends who have allowed me to pester them with questions about their reactions to the Bible.

I am indebted to my son, Gavin, for his constant help and encouragement.

Introduction

Some months ago, the newsagent friend who had supplied me with newspapers and periodicals for the past thirty-five years, decided it was time to retire, and her shop was closed down. The event gave me pause. I had reached the age of eighty-six. Did I really need to go on filling my mind every morning with the details of problems I had long been unable to do anything about? Would it not be better to devote such energy as I have left to the sorting out of one or two of the broader issues which clutter up my mind? If I renounced newspapers, I would have more time to look for help in the many important books I have never opened, and also in those that I have actually read, without definitely deciding what I think about them.

Here I was with a grown-up family of children and grandchildren, and even a great-grandson already fourteen years old, and yet myself with no satisfactory sense of being fully grown-up, since I was so uneasily conscious of unfinished business. That acute French writer, Paul Valéry, remarks somewhere that we should have two lives: the first to be gone through as an apprenticeship, the second to be lived as the real thing. For better or for worse, the unknown power that created us did not order matters in that way. However, I could perhaps round off my single span by making a last little show of effort. There and then, I took a vow of abstention from newspapers and periodicals until further notice.

While I was casting about for a suitable theme or text with which to inaugurate my new routine, the choice was unexpectedly made for me. Through the post arrived a large, brand-new French translation of the Bible. I had heard it advertised on the French radio as representing a major fresh linguistic approach. I had asked for it on an impulse, without foreseeing the effect it would produce. As soon as I opened the English Bible to start comparing it with the French, memories came flooding back of the hours of puzzled boredom it had inflicted on me in childhood and early adolescence – especially the Old Testament, against which, as I now realized, I still harboured a grievance; in fact I was surprised at the strength of the feeling. To confirm or dispel this grievance could be part of the business awaiting completion.

. . . .

At the elementary school, at the grammar school, at Sunday school and in the Primitive Methodist Chapel, excerpts from the Bible were ceremoniously read aloud, but never, as I remember, with any explanatory gloss. No sermon ever queried the Bible, nor did that most excruciating of grammar-school lessons, "religious instruction." The masters who were supposed to teach it were completely at a loss. One or two were ex-public schoolboys of the type that used to be called "muscular Christians" – decent enough fellows, but with a perfectly conventional, wooden approach. It was taken for granted that the biblical text, whatever book it came from, was Holy Writ, and therefore simply to be repeated aloud without debate.

I felt it would be tactless to put up a hand to ask why, if it was common practice for God to speak to Moses, and sometimes "face to face as a man speaketh unto his friend," he had ceased to do so in the case of the leaders and preachers of the modern world. Or why, if Jesus could feed the five thousand on one occasion, it did not occur to him to solve the general problem of poverty and hunger at a stroke. Knowing myself to be incurably literal-minded, I held my peace.

I have often wondered why I was totally devoid of what the French call *la bosse de la révérence*, and particularly of the bump of reverence for religion that distinguishes so many respectable people. My father in his early years was a Wesleyan local preacher, and later a militant Christian Socialist. He died young, after a long illness, and I never had a chance to talk to him. I inherited a second-hand copy of the thirty-ninth edition of Cruden's Concordance, bought by the original owner in 1876, *The Imitation of Christ* by Thomas-à-Kempis, a present from a lady with whom my father had once been involved; (it was a strange choice of book on her part; perhaps his ardour had been chilled by a maxim on page 12: "Be not familiar with any woman; but commend all good women in general to God."), and *The Labour Church Hymn and Tune Book* (1912); it covers the gamut of belief from the religious to the secular, from "Lead, kindly light" to "The People's Flag is deepest red." My mother was a strong-minded country-woman, a simple deist but not a chapel-goer who, during her long widowhood, knelt at her bedside, with her loosened bun hanging down the back of her night-dress, to say the Lord's Prayer. How, with such parents, could I be a miscreant?[1] I had no difficulty in accepting their moral principles ("Do unto others as you would be done by", "Take other people as you find them", "Be beholden to no man", etc.) without feeling that they needed the backing of a fallacious supernatural entity.

---

[1] Some years ago, an acquaintance told me that he had found a reference, in Sydney Smith's diaries, to a certain Weightman, who was the last person in England to be officially burnt alive for heresy, in 1612. I have always felt warmly disposed towards this homonymous unfortunate, supposing him to be a kindred spirit whom I should salute across the centuries. But on checking recently, I was disappointed to discover that Edward Weightman or Wightman, far from being a non-believer, was an over-believer, a deranged Baptist. He is said to have been convinced, among other things, of being a reincarnation of Elijah, the prophet who is mainly remembered for his supposed departure heavenwards in a chariot of fire. Whether Elijah or Edward got to heaven, we do not know. All we can be sure of is that where Edward had been, there remained a pile of ashes in Litchfield.

At first, I was embarrassed by my disbelief. I felt I was abnormal, because there was a gap in my mind where belief in God should have been. Then I reflected that if there were a God, He, She or *x* would understand that I could not help thinking my thoughts according to my temperament, which was a 'given', not something I had chosen. If I were godless, it was "God" who had made me so. Yet my literal-mindedness did not prevent me from enjoying fantasy, provided it had no dogmatic, metaphysical pretensions. One of my favourite poems has always been the eerie nursery-rhyme about the witch's ascent to Heaven: "There was an old woman tossed up in a basket, Ninety times as high as the moon…"

Similarly, despite my general antipathy to religion, odds and ends of biblical phrases stuck in my memory, and kept repeating themselves because of the peculiar charm of the words. They were not necessarily 'important' phrases; why, for instance, should I delight in "We have a little sister, and she hath no breasts"[2] or "Tell it not in Gath, publish it not in the streets of Askelon, lest the daughters of the Philistines rejoice"? The pleasure was purely linguistic; it had nothing to do with faith, to which my mind was resolutely closed from the age of twelve or thirteen.

· ·

When, through a series of flukes, I was later transferred to a different setting, and eventually at the age of twenty-three, found myself earning my living in the French language, I had to prise my mind open again to cater for the phenomenon of Catholicism in French history and culture. I was greatly impressed by a young Catholic colleague of my own age who had spent some time in England, and

---

[2] I suspect the secret lies in the archaic 'hath', which provides a phonetic cushion avoiding 'has no breasts'.

was exasperated by what he considered to be the lukewarm atmosphere of English religious life. *"Où est le scandale du christianisme en Angleterre?"* he exclaimed indignantly. He was using the word *'scandale'* in a positive sense; he meant the glorious irrationality, the exciting gamble, of faith; *credo quia absurdum.* And, to my surprise, on reading the works of some passionate modern French believers, such as Léon Bloy, Georges Bernanos and Simone Weil, I had intimations of how thrilling it might be to convince myself that there is a bridge between the here and now and the ineffable Beyond. But these intimations never lasted very long. I could never bring myself to think of Jesus as *Notre Seigneur,* any more than as "Our Lord". I even found the terms embarrassing, as if they violated some irreducible honesty of my consciousness or conscience. For me, Jesus remained an abstract, impalpable figure, a sort of Good King Wenceslas, admittedly much more highly developed, but essentially of the same mythic nature.

On the other hand, I felt immediately at home in the secular, post-Enlightenment tradition, which constitutes at least half of French culture. When I was young, it seemed to bring the relief of a great clarification after the intellectual chiaroscuro of England. Later, I had to admit that the French post-Enlightenment tradition is not without aberrations of its own. But I have never wavered in the conviction that, at its best, it has the virtue of being completely open-minded; it treats the mystery of life respectfully as a mystery, without forcing it artificially into any dogmatic framework.

1

Renewing Acquaintance with the Bible

The Bible was a major book with which I had never come to terms, and had never read consecutively. Here I had it in a new French version, a huge volume of over three thousand pages, including the Apocrypha, commentaries, an explanatory glossary of Hebrew and Greek terms, maps and other aids to comprehension. I could tackle it without getting lost in the dense forest of biblical exegesis. This vade mecum would be enough for me[3]: an up-to-date scholarly edition, six years in the making and the combined work of no less than forty-seven linguistic experts and littérateurs. It would surely solve some of the queries that had lingered in my mind since childhood. I had no pretentious ambition in commenting on so

---

[3] This did not prove quite true. As I shall explain in due course, the Bayard Version did not face up squarely to all the difficulties, and I had to supplement it with another French translation, *La Bible de Jérusalem* (1974), an impressive collaborative volume produced by thirty Catholic specialists under the direction of *L'Ecole biblique de Jérusalem*. For the sake of convenience, I shall refer to this version in English as the Jerusalem Bible.

established a monument as the Bible; my aim was simply to give a belated airing to my long-standing recalcitrance. I was encouraged by the circumstance that, at first sight, the volume did not seem to come from any markedly partisan source, either pro- or anti- religious. In his Introduction, Frédéric Boyer, the general editor, emphasises the extremely complicated history of the various texts in various languages, which were put together piecemeal over the centuries to form the strange miscellany known as the Bible. He makes no claim for it as being "revealed," nor, on the other hand, does he allow himself any ironical comments on the fairy-tale absurdities, such as Jonah's ability to use the whale as his personal submarine, or the more than doubtful logistics of Noah's Ark. His stated aim is to respect the peculiarity of each book and, through the collaboration in each case of a linguist and a literary stylist, to ensure that the tone is not ironed out into staid academic language, as has often been the case in previous French versions. For a first tasting, I turned to the Song of Songs (8.8): –

Nous avons une sœur
Petite
et sans seins

and then to Samuel II, i, 20: –

Silence à Gat
Pas un mot dans les rues d'Ashqelôn
Les Philistines seraient trop contentes
Quelle joie pour ces filles d'incirconcis!

These snippets are promising. The first is less touching than the English; because it replaces the affectionate "little sister" by the more literal "sister, small in size." The second is excellent, racy and with nice variations in syntax. Both are improvements on the Jerusalem Bible, which shows little feeling for rhythm: –

Notre sœur est petite: elle n'a pas les seins formés

...

Ne le publiez pas à Gat,
Ne l'annoncez pas dans les rues d'Ashqelôn,
Que ne se réjouissent les filles des Philistins,
Que n'exultent les filles d'incirconcis!

"*Que ne se réjouissent*" is particularly 'chewy' and clumsy, but in religious writing, meaning – if there is a meaning – should be more important than beauty of style, which, when it exists, is a bonus.

In the case of very old texts, such as Genesis, meaning may present a special problem. If the basic concepts are uncertain, and moreover juxtaposed with little or none of the explanatory syntactic tissue we are used to in the modern languages, decipherment is a delicate operation, usually involving a degree of invention. I suspect there may be some very ancient Chinese or Egyptian texts, which are beyond interpretation, because the meaning is so remote that it has evaporated. This is not quite the case in Genesis, but one can see how tenuous the hold on meaning is. On opening the Bayard Version which, as Boyer has told us, aims at fidelity to the style of the original, this is what we find: –

Premiers
Dieu crée ciel et terre
terre vide solitude
noir au-dessus des fonds
souffle de Dieu
mouvements au-dessus des eaux
First (things ?)
God creates heaven and earth
land empty solitude
black above the depths
breath of God
movements above the waters

These six lines are presumably following the disjointed syntax of the ancient Hebrew. Not knowing the language, I can have no direct conception of their meaning, or of the poetic force of the original, if it has any. The English Authorised Version renders the passage in the following well-known words: —

> In the beginning God created the heaven and the earth. And the earth was without form and void, and darkness was upon the face of the deep, and the Spirit of God moved upon the face of the waters.[4]

This is a beautiful piece of English prose, harmonious and authoritative in tone; "Darkness was upon the face of the deep and the Spirit of God moved upon the face of the waters" has a sort of creative urge. The text, however, has no "meaning," in the sense that it tells us nothing informative about the creation of the world. It is solemn, poetic trumpeting about matters beyond human ken, but, as such, satisfactory.

The Jerusalem Bible presents a similar, but not absolutely identical, text: —

> *Au commencement, Dieu créa le ciel et la terre. Or, la terre était vide et vague, les ténèbres couvraient l'abîme, un vent de Dieu tournoyait sur les eaux.*

This is less impressive than the English, chiefly because "*un vent de Dieu tournoyait sur les eaux*" (went round and round on the waters) is less strongly and smoothly purposeful than "the Spirit of God moved upon the face of the waters." The French wind seems to be going nowhere. At the same time, *un vent de Dieu* lacks the dignity of "the Spirit of God." It might even make a schoolboy snigger, because *un vent*, in the singular and preceded by the indefinite article, also has the meaning of what is politely referred to as *un bruit incongru. Un vent de Dieu* could be naughtily sacrilegious, like the popular name of

---

[4] The Revised Version changes only one expression: "without form" becomes "waste." I cannot see this as an improvement, because "waste" suggests something which once had a form and then lost it, whereas at this stage the earth has not yet found a form.

a well-known sweet dessert – *des pets de nonne.*

Fortunately, it is only in the early part of Genesis that the reader of the Bayard Version will need to look at a traditional version in parallel to see how these specifically linguistic difficulties have usually been dealt with. Later, the syntax becomes much less jagged, and the obscurities arise more from the gaps, contradictions and puzzles in the narrative itself. But it is interesting to see in what a dim, linguistic twilight the Bible actually begins.

Strictly speaking, Boyer's ambition to retain the individuality of each book is utopian, because every translation involves a double compromise: between the ancient language and the modern one, which may be as different as chalk and cheese, and between the sensibility of the ancient author and that of the translator, who has grown up in a different world. However, this having been said, I would add that, after looking at a good part of the text, I conclude that the most valiant attempt has been made to square the circle.

2
An Ambiguous Undertaking

On another level, it is odd that Boyer, while stating his linguistic aim quite clearly, makes no mention of the promoters of this new publishing venture. It is a joint Franco-Canadian production, printed in France and published simultaneously by Bayard in Paris and Médiaspaul in Montreal. Six years' work by forty-seven contributors and the printing of a volume of 3,000 pages must have cost a lot of money, but no institution or foundation is thanked for financial help. It may be significant that some of the contributors work in Catholic establishments, more particularly in Canada, but their religious allegiance, if they have any, is not stated. Can the enterprise have been sponsored by the Catholic Church in its two national branches? Possibly, but why then, on the first fly-leaf, does *La Commission doctrinale des Evêques de France* issue a warning, although in the most discreet of small print? The text is not to be used for liturgical purposes, and the Commission reserves judgement on its *fidélité profonde à la révélation divine* – its basic respect for divine revelation. If it is sponsored by the two ecclesiastical hierarchies, there must be something of a rift between them, but why does the reservation come from the French side, when the Canadian hierarchy is usually thought to be the more conservative? For the moment, then, this huge volume is a sort of Trojan horse; we cannot be sure whether it carries believers or non-believers in its belly. However, we shall soon see.

In addition to Frédéric Boyer's general Introduction, there are also two separate ones to the Old and New Testaments, the first by Jean-Pierre Prévost, the second by André Myre. They both begin by amplifying the theme already touched upon by Boyer, namely the difficulty, not to say the impossibility, of identifying the origins of the Biblical texts. None of them is pure and authentic in the sense that there is an original manuscript by a known author. Unlike the Koran, they do not constitute a unified composition that was said to be dictated by God, through the agency of the angel Gabriel. They emerged anonymously from the distant past as a heterogeneous collection of writings that have been put together in different ways at different times. It is probably common knowledge that the New Testament began as an oral tradition which passed from Aramaic to Greek, and that the unknown individuals who first set down the story in the original, long-lost manuscripts, had no direct personal knowledge of Jesus, who had died many years before. André Myre points out forcibly that there is a distinction to be made between Jesus of Nazareth, about whom nothing is known for certain, and Jesus Christ, the great persona fashioned subsequently by the Church, on the basis of the Greek gospels and epistles.

It is perhaps less well-known, as Jean-Pierre Prévost explains, that the origins of the books of the Old Testament are equally ambiguous. They are not purely Hebrew, but come out of a long-established Middle-Eastern tradition – Mesopotamian, Sumerian, Egyptian, etc. – which left its mark on them. As is the case of the New Testament, the canonical version was put together over a long period and the editing, again like that of the New Testament, leaves much to be desired, at least from the modern point of view. The narrative sequence is sporadic, with gaps and inexplicable repetitions. Jean-

Pierre Prévost singles out several of these peculiarities and on leafing through the text, one can spot many more.

I am struck, for instance, by the absence of details concerning certain characters. Consider the case of the Queen of Sheba, one of the famous romantic queens of mythic history. The French writer, André Malraux, risked his life as a young man in a hare-brained aerial attempt to discover the site of her lost capital city. I sometimes suspect that she has benefited from a possible confusion in the popular mind between her encounter with Solomon and the dramatic conjunction of Antony and Cleopatra. Handel, of course, gave her a boost with the splendidly assured music of "The arrival of the Queen of Sheba." But when you refer back to the text, she is a disappointment. Her story is told twice in exactly the same prosaic terms in *Kings* I and *Chronicles* II. She comes to Solomon as one celebrity visiting another and "to prove him with hard questions." He answers them apparently to her satisfaction, but since we are not told what the questions and the answers were, we can neither appreciate her acumen nor profit from Solomon's famous wisdom. She says what a great man he is, she praises his splendid household, and declares what a great God his God must be. They exchange lavish gifts, and she departs. The episode sounds like a pro-Solomon publicity stunt, a state visit with an incidental salute to the Jewish God, comparable to the modern ceremony of laying a wreath on the tomb of the Unknown Soldier.

While I was expressing my regret at the elusiveness of the Queen of Sheba, I did not know that officials at the British Museum were preparing an exhibition entitled "Queen of Sheba, treasures of Ancient Yemen," sponsored by Barclay's Bank and with the collaboration of the Ministry of Culture of the Yemenite Republic. The catalogue is a substantial illustrated book[5]. It confirms that

---

[5] The British Museum Press, 2002.

nothing definite is known about the lady, except that she was also referred to as Bilqîs, or was confused with someone else of that name. The growth of the myth seems to have gone hand in hand with biblical illustration since ancient times. It flourished particularly in the Western world during the orientalist vogue of the nineteenth century, which was stimulated both by archaeological discoveries and by the French interest in Eastern eroticism. It reached a peak with the academic painter, Sir John Poynter (1836-1919), who devoted several years to his monumental canvas, *The Queen of Sheba's Visit to Solomon*; society ladies attended balls in supposedly Sheba costumes, more heavily ornamented than the revealing royal accoutrements favoured by the painter. It is an interesting historical irony that a queen, and a mythic one at that, should now act as a valuable cultural and even political prop for a modern republic.

There is an odd extension to the Sheba story, which is not mentioned in the Bible. Bilqîs-Sheba of Yemen was somehow associated, or confused, with Bilqîs-Mekena, Queen of Northern Ethiopia. She too, it is said, paid a visit to Jerusalem, which was less formal but more fruitful than Sheba's. Solomon generously impregnated both her and her handmaiden who, on their return to Ethiopia, gave birth to two half-brothers, a convenient arrangement, since the boys grew up as companions; there is a folk illustration which shows them, side by side, proudly clutching the sticks with which they played the Ethiopian equivalent of hockey. The Queen's son, Menelik, is said to have visited Solomon as a young man. He eventually founded the Solomonic dynasty of Ethiopia, the last representative of which was Haile Selassie[6].

---

[6] Through a curious concatenation of circumstances, connected with a British family who had property in London and Ethiopia, only five minute's walk from where I am sitting in London, there is a Menelik Road, which was named after this supposed son of Solomon.

. . . .

However, one of the greatest mysteries surrounds the central figure of Moses. If Pharaoh had decreed the slaughter of all male Jewish babies how did Pharaoh's daughter manage to bring him up in the royal household as her adopted son? If he grew up speaking Egyptian (Jethro's daughters refer to him as "the Egyptian"), how did he learn Hebrew and become acquainted with the Hebrew tradition? There is a whole early life-story missing here. The tale of the babe in the bulrushes is very pretty, but perhaps it is no truer than the old fib that babies were born under cabbage-leaves. Suppose Pharaoh's daughter was concealing a clandestine affair with an Egyptian lover, or with a Joseph who could not resist the pressure exercised by a princess, more powerful than Potiphar's wife. In the first case, Moses would not be Jewish at all; in the second, he would be a half-Jew who discovered his Jewishness in early manhood. Such cases occur in real life; I personally know of two. There is a blank here, which makes Moses as enigmatic a figure as the carpenter's son who became Jesus Christ.

These obscurities and discrepancies would not matter at all, if the Bible were classed as myth, that is, as a collection of stories about humanity not to be taken as an actual historical record, but to be read for the sake of their human interest and their possible symbolic significance. Had it been presented to me as such in childhood or early adolescence, I would have had no difficulty with it. What was irksome was to be expected to pretend it was the Truth, therefore different in kind from, and superior to, all other mythic systems. And despite the supposed increase of scepticism in the modern world, there are still millions of people who believe in the truth of their unique mythic system: the orthodox Christians, the orthodox Jews and the orthodox Muslims, and all the subdivisions into which they are divided. Again, this would not matter if orthodoxies could co-exist peacefully; but they inevitably breed gratuitous concepts of right and wrong.

23

Since Boyer seemed so objective in his general introduction, and since Prévost and Myre are so frank about the uncertainties of the biblical text, I went on reading, and assuming that they would eventually conclude: "Yes, all this is myth, but it has interesting non-supernatural implications." Imagine my surprise when I realised that they were avoiding the word "myth" and, in their different ways, were about to reassert a dependence on faith. Actually, had I paid more attention to the lay-out of the book before I read the introductions, I would have noticed that the affirmation of faith is visible from the start. The traditional terms, *l'Ancient Testament* and *le Nouveau Testament* are replaced by the terms *L'Alliance* and *La Nouvelle Alliance*. This is to emphasise a point which is presented as axiomatic: we are expected to believe that there is no discrepancy between the two Testaments; they form a sequence illustrating the two stages of God's covenant with man. Referring to the Old Testament, Prévost asserts confidently: –

> *La Tora…inscrit le grand livre de la Révélation sous le signe de la pluralité*. (The Tora puts the mark of plurality on the great book of Revelation.)

By this I take him to mean that there were several privileged interlocutors who spoke with God – Abraham, Isaac, Jacob, etc., and above all Moses, *l'homme du face-à-face avec Dieu* (standing face to face with God), who was the first in importance of the early interlocutors, but the last in chronological sequence.

This assumption blandly ignores the central problem of the "Revelation." Did God actually speak to man in those remote times, or were the prophets and other individuals who claimed to converse with God in the grip of a collective delusion which made them assume that the promptings of their own minds were the voice of

God? It is true that the expressions "the Lord said" or "the Lord spoke" occur so frequently in the Old Testament that the reader may well be lulled or hypnotised into accepting "the Lord" as a real character, who was vocal in ancient times, but has fallen silent in later history. But, on reflection, can any rational being agree that this is, or was, the case? Does Jean-Pierre Prévost believe it himself? If so, he should have stated the fact boldly, since it runs counter to linguistic science. I doubt whether any modern ecclesiastic would be prepared to say: "Yes, I believe that there has been a clean break in history. God once spoke openly to man; now he no longer does so." Such an assertion would be extremely useful, because it would provoke a much-needed debate on the modes of language-use in the Bible.

Meanwhile, I work on the assumption that all the words in the Bible come from human minds. Hence all the obscurities and contradictions in the text. There can be no covenant, because man cannot strike a bargain with the transcendent; there is no concrete partner to append his signature or to pledge his word. Besides, it seems to have been forgotten for the moment that the imaginary covenant, as presented in the Old Testament, is not between God and man; it is between God and the Jewish people. It is a private arrangement, from which the mass of humanity is excluded. It is strange that various Gentile communities should have appropriated it, as if it were relevant to themselves. How this happened is explained to some extent in the Acts of the Apostles.

. . . .

It is disappointing that the Bayard Version should completely shirk this vital issue of the validity of the language used by the prophets. The Jerusalem Bible has at least the virtue of approaching the problem directly. In its general introduction to the prophetic books, it recognises that prophesying was a characteristic common to all the major religions of the remote past: –

A des degrés divers et sous des formes variables, les grandes religions de l'Antiquité ont eu des inspirés qui prétendaient parler au nom de leur Dieu.. (To different degrees and in various forms, the major religions of Antiquity had enthusiasts who claimed to speak on behalf of their god.)

Even before, and during, the times of the prophets officially recognised by inclusion in the Bible, there were groups of turbulent mystics who considered themselves as representatives of Jehovah: –

… ils ont parfois des comportements étranges, ils peuvent passer par des états psychologiques anormaux, mais ces manifestations extraordinaires ne sont jamais l'essentiel chez les prophètes dont la Bible a retenu l'action et les paroles. Ceux-ci se distinguent nettement des exaltés des anciennes confréries. (… they sometimes behave strangely, and may exhibit abnormal psychological symptoms, but these extraordinary characteristics are never paramount in the case of the prophets whose activities and declarations are recorded in the Bible. The latter can be clearly differentiated from the fanatics of the ancient brotherhoods.)

Is this generalisation quite true? Take the case of Elijah, the Tishbite. He is fed by ravens, he creates a miraculous source of food for the woman who treats him charitably, he raises her son from the dead, he challenges the god, Baal, to a fire-raising competition and wins easily by calling down fire from heaven, after which he slaughters the priests of Baal wholesale, not to mention three successive detachments of soldiers sent against him by the king of Samaria. Finally, he enjoys his own private assumption; he goes heavenwards in a chariot of fire drawn by fiery horses, leaving behind his magic mantle, which has the power to divide the waters. Surely, these activities must count as *des manifestations extraordinaires* – some of them are miracles – but the Jerusalem Bible does not say so. Elijah's disciple, Elisha, who inherited the magic mantle, was also a wonder-worker: he cleansed a contaminated spring with a sprinkling of salt, cured a woman's infertility and raised her son from the dead. At the same time, he was no model of restraint; when a group of youngsters called after him: "Go up, thou bald head!", he caused she-bears to came out of the wood and tear "forty and two" of them to pieces. He also punished a disobedient servant by infecting him and his family with leprosy.

However, the Jerusalem Bible continues serenely with a dogmatic statement that I must quote in full: –

… tout vrai prophète a conscience qu'il n'est qu'un instrument, que les mots qu'il profère sont à la fois siens et non siens. Il a la conviction inébranlable qu'il a reçu une parole de Dieu et qu'il doit la communiquer. Cette conviction est fondée sur l'expérience mystérieuse, disons mystique, d'un contact immédiat avec Dieu. Il arrive, comme on l'a dit, que cette emprise divine provoque extérieurement des manifestations "anormales," mais ce n'est qu'un accident, comme chez les grands mystiques. Par contre, comme pour les mystiques encore, on doit affirmer que cette intervention de Dieu dans l'âme du prophète met celui-ci dans un état psychologique "supra-normal." Le nier serait abaisser l'esprit prophétique au niveau de l'inspiration du poète, ou des illusions des pseudo-inspirés.

(… every true prophet realises that he is only an instrument, that the words he utters are at once his own and not his own. He has the unshakeable conviction that he has received the word of God and must pass it on. His conviction is based on the mysterious, or better, mystic, experience of direct contact with God. As has already been said, it can happen that this possession by the divine produces outward symptoms of "abnormality." But this is accidental, as in the case of the great mystics. On the other hand, and again as in the case of the great mystics, it must be affirmed that the entry of God into the soul of the prophet puts the latter into a supra-normal psychological state. To deny this is to reduce the prophetic spirit to the level of poetic inspiration or the delusions of the pseudo-inspired.)

Setting aside considerations of "abnormality" or "extraordinary symptoms," this is a gratuitous assertion of the validity of the "prophetic spirit" as an objective phenomenon in itself. No evidence is offered. The belief rests entirely on the subjective conviction of the prophet himself, which has to be taken on trust. It does not further understanding, but calls for an act of faith, which avoids the issue. I conclude that the editors of the Jerusalem Bible, like Jean-Pierre Prévost in the Bayard Version, are blind to the fact that the phenomenon of prophecy as it occurs in the Old Testament, is an unsolved linguistic problem.

. . . .

Myre's retreat into belief is even more curious than Prévost's. We have already seen that he makes a clear distinction between Jesus of Nazareth, the problematic figure about whom nothing is known for certain, and Jesus Christ, the entity created by the Church. Jesus Christ is surely a myth, if ever there was one. But Myre goes even further in undermining the authenticity of the Revelation by pointing out that there are five thousand manuscripts of various parts of the New Testament that exegetes are still trying to reconcile with each other: —

> Cela peut surprendre mais au sens strict la Bible n'existe pas.
> Chaque époque, chaque culture, se doit d'en décider le mot-à-mot
> avant de la traduire pour tenter de la rendre accessible.

> (It may seem surprising, but, strictly speaking *the* Bible does not
> exist. Each epoch, each culture, must make up its mind about
> the actual wording of the text, before translating it to make it
> more comprehensible.)

This can only mean that the Revelation is not a truth handed down once and for all; instead of being stable, it is a sort of guessing game based on the uncertainties of language, and which goes on from generation to generation. It follows that the so-called "New Covenant" is subject to endless revision. It is obvious that what is called "faith" evolves in time. One only has to reflect a moment to realise that if the Grand Inquisitor and Calvin could come back tomorrow, both the present Pope and the Archbishop of Canterbury would be burnt at the stake as heretics. Does this not prove that, at any stage and in whatever religion, precise conviction about dogma is a deceptive and dangerous certainty, which may distort morality instead of supporting it?

In his conclusion, André Myre rather plays down the importance of the "New Covenant." He puts his faith in the Apocalypse, the last book of the New Testament, which was written towards the end of the first century and expresses, in violent and often obscure imagery, the indignation of the early Christian communities at their persecution by the Roman Empire, which is characterised as "The Beast." For Myre, the protest against the Beast is the symbol of Christian hope in the face of evil: –

Vivre, c'est résister dans l'espérance du triomphe ultime de la vie. La Nouvelle Alliance se tait, après avoir ainsi tracé le chemin.

(To live, is to go on resisting in the hope of the ultimate triumph of life. The New Covenant falls silent, after indicating the road to be followed.)

The road seems to be that of pious, gratuitous faith. What meaning can be given to the expression "the triumph of life"? In this world, there can be no such triumph; life is transitory, and its necessary corollary is death[7]. It is true that there can be an ever-renewed struggle against the various forms of evil, some reducible, others

---

[7] Paul Valéry has a whimsical epigram on this theme: –
L'individu, machine à se conserver, porte sa condamnation à disparaître sous les espèces de l'appareil sexuel, chargé des énergies de substitution, de remplacement. (cont. overleaf)

intractable. As for life in some other world, we can have no possible conception of what it might be. Myre is just rounding off his introduction with phatic religious parlance.

Frédéric Boyer seemed to announce a well-intentioned, scholarly and purely secular edition of the Bible. Jean-Pierre Prévost and André Myre are schizophrenic in the sense that their scholarship is laced with religious assumptions, that are in glaring contradiction with it. We see now that the Trojan horse contains a motley collection of believers or half-believers.

Ces organes lui chantent : Frère, il faut mourir.
(The individual, a self-preserving organism, carries the doom of extinction with him in the guise of his sexual equipment, primed with the wherewithal for substitution and replacement. His genitalia sing to his inward ear: Brother, you must die.)

3

That Unpleasant Person, God

It has often been assumed, I think, that the transition from the many pagan gods of Greece and Rome to the single God of the Jews and the Christians, was a cultural advance. After the confusions of polytheism, with a multiplicity of gods and goddesses, that is, an oligarchy of supernatural creatures, quarrelling amongst themselves and intervening capriciously in human affairs, it might seem a relief to conceive of a single God solely responsible for creation. Precisely because it is *his* creation, he could logically be expected to administer it in the best possible way, he himself being, of course, the only judge of what is possible. If life could have been better, God would have made it so. This is the Leibnizian, or neo-Leibnizian assumption that Voltaire pokes fun at in *Candide* through the character of Pangloss, who, after every new disaster repeats: *Tout est pour le mieux dans le meilleur des mondes possibles.* There is a flaw in the assumption; God cannot be at once all-powerful, and yet subject to a still greater power which determines the limits of the possible for him.

As far as I know, this difficulty does not arise in paganism, because Zeus and Jupiter are not all-powerful in the absolute sense: each of them is only *primus inter pares*. Arguments and rivalries occur between the gods and goddesses; they have their different domains to represent and defend. They have personalities and various functions. In short, they are like magnified human beings, and their interlocking actions impose no dogmatic pattern on the background of Fate. There is no lack of cruelty in the pagan world, but there is also liveliness and diversity.

What depressed me most about the Old Testament was the terrible sensation of claustrophobia that it engendered, through the all-invasive presence of the single God. How unfortunate to have only one God, and he a bully, not to say a tyrant! God was a cross supervisor, brooding over the world and ready to take offence at every turn. He and his prophets spent most of their time complaining and threatening. The dominant emotion in many of the chapters of the Bible was appreciation of power and riches in this world, which God awarded or took away according to his whim. The bonus for complete obedience was the promise of many descendents, who would be well-treated, provided they were submissive in their turn. If not, woe unto them!

It is not too much to say that I hated the concept of this God-Person, who demanded complete obedience and adoration. I could not help thinking that if there were a Creator – and we must assume that there is/was a creative entity of some kind – it would be beneath its dignity to expect adoration from human beings. What significance could such adoration possibly have? "Hello, humans, I am your Creator! Admire me! Three cheers for Myself!" Whatever the power behind the universe, how could one conceive of it in such a reductionist form as a Person with susceptibilities? To my mind, the pagan acceptance of the inscrutable background of Fate made better sense than any orthodoxy involving a personal god.

The Bible puts the relationship between the Jews and their God in a particularly strong form: –

Ye are the children of the Lord Your God...

For thou art an holy people unto the Lord thy

God, and the Lord hath chosen thee to be a
peculiar people unto himself, above all
peoples that are upon the face of the earth. (Deut. 7.6)

Despite this bold assertion, many other communities think, or
have thought, that they have a God peculiar to themselves. As I write,
it happens to be Jubilee Day in Britain, the fiftieth anniversary of the
reign of the Queen, Head of the Church of England. Anglicans and
Non-Conformists are singing "God Save the Queen," but I do not
suppose that they feel their God to be the same as the God of the
Catholic IRA, and vice versa. The USA is sometimes referred to as
"God's own country," and God was earnestly invoked as a patron
after the disaster of the World Trade Centre. France traditionally
thought of herself as *la fille aînée de l'Eglise*, the eldest daughter of the
Church, that is the next in line after the Papacy. Louis XIV,
convinced that, as King, he was on a par with God, was offended
when God allowed the last years of his reign to be clouded by disaster:
"God ought to remember what I have done for Him." (He had
conscientiously persecuted the Huguenots.) The nineteenth-century
Russian poet, Tiutchev, wrote a beautiful little poem entitled "Holy
Russia", which, like William Blake's "Jerusalem", presents his native
country as being particularly dear to Christ. Even the otherwise Godless Nazis, so I am told, had *Gott mit uns* inscribed on their belts. The
Palestinian suicide-bombers, imitating Japanese Kamikazi pilots who
died for their Emperor-God, are sacrificing themselves in the name of
Allah. The phenomenon is universal, and, like an epidemic, manifests
itself here and there at different times and with different intensities.
It is endemic throughout the Old Testament, although we are never
given any explanation of why the Creator needed to have a Chosen
People. Why should he take a particular interest in only one part of
his creation?

What some people might call Fate or Chance is presented in the
Old Testament as the history of this interactive relationship between

the Jewish people and their personal God, with God taking most of the initiative, particularly from the time of the coming out of Egypt, which is constantly referred back to as God's great demonstration of favour towards the Jews. Actually, the relationship really dates from the so-called covenant between God and Abraham, when God, as Moses keeps repeating, swore to bring the Jews to the land he had promised to their forefathers, the land flowing with milk and honey, containing "great and goodly cities" ... "and houses full of good things." (Deut 6.10). The exodus, although a favour to the Jews, was planned to end with a holocaust of others of God's creatures: –

When the Lord thy God shall bring thee into the land whither thou goest to possess it, and shall cast out many nations before thee, the Hittite and the Gorgashite, and the Amorite, and the Canaanite, and the Perizzite and the Hivite, and the Jebesite, seven nations greater and mightier than thou; And when the Lord thy God shall deliver them up before thee, and thou shalt smite them; then thou shalt utterly destroy them; thou shalt make no covenant with them, nor show mercy to them: Neither shalt thou make marriages with them ... (Deut 2.1,2,3).

So, in three short verses, deliberate massacre plus racialism. Subsequently, the story is told entirely from the point of view of the Israelites. We remain ignorant of what the seven nations have done to deserve such treatment, nor do we learn anything about their reaction. It is as if they were beyond the pale of humanity.

But even if we look at things from the point of view of the Jews, the story of the coming out of Egypt is full of strange peculiarities. Why were the Jews in Egypt in the first place? They had taken refuge there, because of a famine in their own country. A famine is a natural disaster, "an act of God." Therefore, God himself was originally responsible for their exile.

At first the Jews were well treated in Egypt, and their numbers increased to such an extent that the native Egyptians began to resent their presence. A cruel Pharaoh came to power and enslaved them. God calls upon Moses to lead the Jews back to their homeland, by now, no doubt, after a long absence, an abstract ideal rather than a precise memory. Moses and Aaron plead with the Pharaoh to let their people go, but God "hardens Pharaoh's heart," so that he refuses his consent more than once. Why did God do this? So that he can demonstrate his power by smiting Egypt with plagues. He boasts about this. Here is a blatantly unethical situation; an entire people is punished because of the attitude of its ruler, and that attitude has been determined by God himself! The narrative gets into this tangle, because God is presented as being all-powerful, while using his power in a way which is both partial and incoherent. Anyone familiar with the satirical farces of Alfred Jarry will be struck by God's similarity to *Le Père Ubu*.

Eventually, God gets his people across Jordan and into the Promised Land, after much suffering and punishment on the way. But he does not leave them there. Finding new reasons to be displeased with them, he allows them to be taken into slavery again at least twice, and eventually, in circumstances beyond the compass of the Old Testament, they are subject to the diaspora. It is true that Ezekiel, one of the most fiery of the prophets, who forecasts the diaspora as a consequence of Israel's misdeeds, also promises that, in the fullness of time, God will return the Jews to their homeland as a shepherd rounds up his wandering sheep. However, we can now see that the sheepfold, having been, in a sense, arbitrarily re-established, is not a place of rest. God has not yet solved the problem of his Chosen People.

. . . .

I was familiar with the casual cruelty of the Old Testament God from an early age. One of my aunts had a large old bible, with full-page, black-and-white illustrations. I can still see Isaac on the altar, trussed like a chicken and Abraham with his knife at the ready. The fact that God cancelled the sacrifice at the last moment did nothing to endear him to me. It was a shoddy device to use the ram caught in the thicket as a stand-in. "Damned unsporting, what!"; God had to have his pound of flesh, even if it was only animal flesh. I was to learn later, of course, that in many barbarous, superstitious communities, it was common practice to sacrifice children, virgins, bringers of bad tidings and scapegoats of all kinds in order to placate the gods, but the fact that barbarism is widespread does not make it any the less barbaric.

During my present reperusal of the Old Testament, I am struck by the extraordinary frequency with which God shows no respect for life when, after all, life might be considered as the central feature of his creation. According to the Book of Genesis, "it repented God that he had made man on earth," and he wiped out all living creatures, humans and animals alike by means of the Flood, as if they had been an unwanted litter of kittens. Oddly enough, he does not make a completely fresh start, but saves enough specimens in the Ark to relaunch the process with the same ingredients. Still more oddly, he never explains what was the nature of the "evil" done by the original humans, who existed between the departure from the Garden of Eden and the generation of Noah. This is a recurrent puzzle in the Biblical story. The Lord constantly foments a feeling of guilt in the Jews by saying that he is displeased with them and will punish them, but the reason for his displeasure may remain obscure; there is not always a Golden Calf to be blamed. Hence the bewilderment that runs through the Psalms. God is a protector at one moment, and an avenger a moment later. The secular mind, of course, sees this as a consequence of trying to interpret the quirks of fate as the deliberate decisions of a personal God. Dispense with the idea of God as a superstition, and you are free to deal with the blows of fate as best you can, unhampered by any feeling of guilt; life may remain tragic, but at least the tragedy is pure.

However, the personal God rampages through the books of the Old Testament. He allows whole human communities to be massacred, or orders them to be massacred or massacres them himself by means of plagues, fire from heaven, or other devices. He is no kinder to animals, although animals, having no moral sense, cannot be said to sin. He institutes elaborate rules concerning their selection for sacrifice, the numbers appropriate for the atonement of different misdeeds, or for the celebration of various ceremonies. Old Testament worship entails a continuous holocaust of animals, with the smell of burning meat going up to God "as a sweet savour."

God is also pedantic about the strict execution of his commands. I have came across some ferocious passages, which I did not know about before, perhaps because they were deemed unsuitable for reading aloud in chapel or in school assembly. Chapter fourteen of Samuel I tells how God, via the prophet Samuel, transmits to Saul, the king of Israel, the message that he must attack the Amalekites, who had been hostile to the Jews when they first came back from Egypt: –

> Now go and smite Amalek, and utterly destroy all that they
> have, and spare them not; but slay both man and woman, infant
> and suckling, ox and sheep, camel and ass.

Saul has the decency to warn another group, the Kenites, who are somehow involved with the Amalekites, that they must get out of the way, and they depart. Saul then sets to with his forces, and utterly destroys the Amalekites. However he happens to take their king, Agag, alive, and his troops, instead of killing all the cattle, select the best and bring them home. The Lord, in a fury, complains to Samuel that Saul has not completed the commission satisfactorily. Samuel, in a fury, comes to see Saul: –

What meaneth this bleating of sheep in mine ears, and the
lowing of the oxen which I hear?

Saul, no doubt putting the best possible face on the matter, explains
that the people have brought back the cattle in order to sacrifice them
"unto the Lord, thy God, in Gilgal." This earns him a sharp rebuke: -

Has the Lord as great delight in burnt offerings and sacrifices, as
in obeying the voice of the Lord? Behold, to obey is better than
sacrifice, and to hearken better than the fat of rams.

Samuel then informs Saul that he is demoted from his kingship,
because of his disobedience, and orders that king Agag should be
brought in: –

And Samuel hewed Agag in pieces before the Lord in Gilgal.

Another barbarous episode, set during the reign of King David,
presents warfare as a sort of sport that kings practise annually at the
appropriate season: –

And it came to pass, at the time of the return of the year when
kings go out to battle, that Joab (the Jewish commander) led
forth the power of the army and wasted the country of the
children of Ammon and came and besieged Rabbah … And
Joab smote Rabbah, and overthrew it.

King David arrives after the siege.

And David took the crown of their king from off his head …
and it was set upon David's head; and he brought forth the spoil
of the siege, exceeding much. And he brought forth the people
that were therein, and cut them with saws and with harrows of
iron, and with axes. And thus did David with all the cities of the
children of Ammon.

I have copied this as a horror story from the Revised Version. It is
essentially the same in the Authorised Version, and is repeated in
Chronicles I.20.3. Being particularly revolted by the awkward and
messy use of saws and harrows as instruments of execution, I decided
to check with the two French versions. Lo and behold, there is no

mention of harrows (*herses*) in either. According to the Bayard Version, David, after taking the crown and the spoil, *réquisitionna les habitants de la ville* and set them to work with saws and axes and at the making of bricks, i.e. he turned them into bondsmen. I would plump for this version, since it sounds more plausible. Consequently, I withdraw the episode as a horror story (unless some reader is soft-hearted enough to feel that enslaving the defeated, although a well-established tradition in the Ancient World, counts as a horror), but I leave it in as an example of the wild uncertainties of the Biblical text. There is no lack of horror stories elsewhere.

In fact, in the very next chapter, after the account of the siege of Rabbah, there is a very curious episode in which David lays himself open to punishment. He instructs his commander, Joab, to carry out a census of the Jewish people[8]. Joab is loth to do this, because "it will be a cause of guilt unto Israel." This is another example of a transgression remaining unexplained. Perhaps there was a superstition about numbering. I remember from my childhood that the sheep-farmers on the Northumbrian moors had a belief that to reveal the precise number of sheep in a flock was sure to bring bad luck. Perhaps some similar belief is in operation here, although quite a lot of numbering goes on in the Old Testament (cf., in particular, the Book of Ezra, chapter two). But Holy Writ abounds in contradictions.

The census takes place, and David is conscious, not so much of

---

[8] The English versions state that it was Satan who inspired David to carry out the census. The Bayard Version has an intriguing but unsatisfactory note to the effect that, in the original source, it was God himself who prompted David to commit the misdeed. Why? you may ask in vain. But, somewhere along the line of descent, "someone" was shocked at the idea of God actually encouraging misbehaviour, and so "*on lui a substitué Satan*". We are left to guess who this *on* was, and who authorised the substitution, and when. If God was testing David by deliberately leading him into temptation, he was not only a jealous God, but an incomprehensibly perverse one, indeed a sort of Satan.

being guilty as of having blundered. God sends him a seer to offer him a choice between punishments. The seer's syntax is rather contorted: –

Either three years of famine; or three months to be consumed before thy foes while that the sword of thine enemies overtaketh thee; or else three days of the sword of the Lord, even pestilence in the land, and the angel of the Lord destroying through all the coasts of Israel.

David opts for "the sword of the Lord": –

So the Lord sent a pestilence upon Israel: and there fell of Israel seventy thousand men.

As in the case of the plagues of Egypt, the Lord's justice is a very blunt instrument, which spares the leader, and wreaks havoc among the innocent.

Perhaps the strangest of all the barbaric episodes is one related to the early days of Moses's mission, just before he leads the Jews out of Egypt. It involves two very confused issues: race and circumcision. We have already seen that the origins of Moses are open to doubt. He is credited with a Jewish mother and a sister who keeps watch to see who will pick him up. There is no mention of his father, and the behaviour of Pharaoh's daughter is suspect. In most royal families, there are rumours of illegitimacy and substitution of babies. Even in respectable England, if I remember rightly, it was still the custom in the early years of the last century for the Home Secretary to take up residence in Buckingham Palace just before a Royal birth, so as to guarantee the authenticity of the proceedings, at least officially.

In the case of Moses, there are two complications, in addition to the central doubt. When he first fled from Egypt as a young man, he took refuge with Jethro, a Bedouin not a Jew, and he married one of Jethro's daughters, by whom he had two children. He had thus "married out," from the Jewish point of view. But, more seriously, before he was taken in charge by Pharaoh's daughter, had he been properly circumcised according to the Jewish rite? In the text, the question remains open.

From a simple reading of the Old Testament narrative, it is difficult to work out exactly what were racial characteristics and what were religious symbols. At times, even membership of the Chosen People seems rather fluid. According to the Jerusalem Bible, circumcision was widely practised in the Ancient World, and it was first linked with the marriage ceremony. Singularly ill-timed, one would have thought, but perhaps the phrase only means that circumcision was part of the rites of passage at puberty, in preparation for marriage at a later stage. But the Structuralist's eye lights up; "A ring of flesh is taken from the bridegroom's penis and symbolically placed on the bride's finger as a metal ring. What a neat balance!" But the Jewish circumcision is not meant to have any connection with sex. It was a symbol of the supposed covenant between God and the Jewish people, and was introduced at the time of Abraham. The official date of the ceremony was fixed at eight days after birth. Abraham himself was rather mature for such an innovation, being then aged ninety-nine. But he went through with it, and so did all the men in his household. However, God's subsequent stipulations about circumcision are not quite clear. It was sometimes extended to servants or bondsmen. Did their racial status remain unaltered, or did they become honorary Jews?

The puzzling episode to which I draw attention concerns Moses, his wife Zipporah and their two sons, who were presumably being brought up as Bedouin, among whom circumcision was fixed at the age of thirteen. When Moses went down into Egypt to join forces with Aaron, he took Zipporah and his two sons with him. Meanwhile, there had been an altercation between the Lord and Pharaoh, and the Lord had threatened to kill Pharaoh's first-born. Then, without any transition, we have the following verses (Ex.4): –

24 And it came to pass on the way at the lodging house that the

Lord met him and sought to kill him.

25 Then Zipporah took a flint and cut off the foreskin of her son, and cast it at his feet.

26 So he let him alone. Then she said: "a bridegroom of blood art thou because of the circumcision."

It is natural to assume that the "him" in verse 24 refers to Pharaoh's son, and that for once the Lord did not carry out his intention to kill. But what is the meaning of Zipporah's behaviour? The Bayard edition, which is continuously disappointing as regards elucidation, leaves the problem unsolved, but there is a glimmer of light in a marginal note to the passage in the Bible of Jerusalem. We have been misled about the identity of the "him." It is Moses that the Lord seeks to kill. How unlikely you will say, since he is about to be entrusted with such an important mission! But the Lord has just remembered that Moses, having had an Egyptian upbringing, may be uncircumcised, or not properly circumcised according to the Jewish rite, and therefore must be destroyed. Zipporah, realising the danger, hurriedly circumcises her son, and smears some of the blood on Moses's private parts ("feet" is a recurrent Hebrew euphemism for "private parts"; cf. Samuel I, 24.3, where "to cover his feet" = "to relieve himself," and also Ruth 3.8). By so doing, she symbolically circumcises Moses as well. This symbolisation is enough to appease the wrath of the Lord, and Moses is saved. In this instance, the Lord is easily satisfied, because the episode would seem to lead to endless casuistical arguments, which the text avoids. What is the validity of the circumcision of a boy, whose mother is a Medianite? Can the symbolic force of the circumcision of the boy be transferred to the father? Here, at the heart of the Old Testament, is a mystery which, to some people may seem important: was Moses properly circumcised or not?

A kind Jewish neighbour has leant me a copy of extracts from the Pentateuch with a commentary from the Jewish point of view. It puts a rather different gloss on the Zipporah episode. God is displeased with Moses on two counts: he was hesitating about the mission God wished to entrust to him; he was delaying the circumcision of his younger (?) son, perhaps under the influence of Jethro and Zipporah, since the Bedouin postponed circumcision until the age of thirteen. "Sought to kill him" is not to be taken literally; it is "an anthropomorphic way of saying that Moses fell into a serious illness." Zipporah performs the circumcision herself, "Moses being disabled by illness." She casts the bleeding skin at the feet of Moses "to connect him with what she has done." It is the child, not Moses, who is "the bridegroom of blood." According to the commentator, Ibn Esra, Zipporah is, in effect, saying to the child: "Indeed, thee I might call literally *the bridegroom of blood*, because thou didst nearly cause the death of my husband." But if Moses was in danger of death, the "anthropomorphic way of speaking" was in fact, equivalent to "sought to kill," and Zipporah acted in fear of God. I leave the reader to sort out these various suppositions according to preference. I merely note that the passage, like so many others, has no settled meaning, and that Moses's circumcision remains problematic.

4
Three Heroines

Despite the obscurities of the Old Testament, there is enough that is explicit in it to make it detestable to the secular mind. My reacquaintance with it has exacerbated rather than diminished my dislike, even though the text is crammed with human interest. If I believed in the Jewish God as a reality and not as a baleful figment of the imaginations of the prophets, I would say that it was unfortunate for the Jews that they were selected to be the Chosen People. They were chosen to suffer; they were the whipping boys of the Lord, as will become even clearer, I fear, from a consideration of the stipulations surrounding the Ten Commandments, as well as from the Psalms and the Book of Job[9].

But let us take a rest for a while from what has been so far almost purely masculine violence to look at the possibly milder books of the Old Testament named after women: Judith, Esther and Ruth. We know in advance that Judith could hardly have been a believer in non-violence, since there are paintings which show her grasping the severed head of Holophernes by the hair. However, according to the Bayard commentary, she may be a purely emblematic figure with no

---

[9] The best modern literary expression of the pride, anguish and confusion of being Jewish that I have come across is in the novels and other writings of Albert Cohen (1895-1981). They remain mostly untranslated.

foundation in history. She may not have been a real person like Joan of Arc or Charlotte Corday who stabbed Marat in his bath, but more of a symbol, comparable to Boadicea defying the Romans. This is further suggested by the fictitious place-names in the story. Also, her canonical status is unsure. She is included in the Catholic Bible, but relegated to the Apocrypha by the Protestants. The story is Hebrew, but survives only in a Greek translation.

. . . .

The plot is simple. Nabuchodonosor, in his mad attempt to conquer the world, sends his commander, Holophernes, to dominate the West. Holophernes besieges the Jewish town of Bethulia, the key to Jerusalem and cuts off the water supply. The elders of the town, after praying to the Lord, decide that if he does not come to their rescue within five days, they will surrender to the enemy. Judith, a rich and beautiful widow, and a strong-minded woman, vows to change the situation during the five days. She prays still more fervently than the elders, arrays herself in all her finery and, accompanied by a maid-servant carrying their kosher food supply in a bag, approaches the enemy sentinels and offers to reveal a secret way into the town. The sentinels impressed by her charms, take her to Holophernes, who is similarly affected. She asks to be allowed, together with her servant, to continue with her prayers and ritual ablutions outside the camp, particularly in the early morning. The infatuated Holophernes agrees, while at the same time inviting her to a feast in the evening. She accepts and when they are left alone after the feast, and Holophernes falls into a drunken slumber, she cuts off his head with his sword, puts it into the food bag together with the ornamented mosquito-net from his bed, and she and the maid-servant slip out of the camp, back to Bethulia. The head is displayed on the battlements. The demoralised enemy is easily routed and the townspeople praise God and Judith.

As so often happens, the details are left vague. Did Judith drug Holophernes? Would an experienced commander not be used to raping his victims before succumbing to drink? Did he demand his due? If Judith prostituted herself, did she sin, or was her heroism enhanced? It is perhaps significant that she was an experienced widow, not a virgin. The commentary in the Bayard Version raises no awkward questions. The moral of the story, we are told, is that you should not always wait for God to act. He helps those who help themselves, provided they have faith in him.

. . . .

Esther is a more passive example of the power of female beauty. When the story opens, she has recently became queen to Ahasuerus, King of the Persians. Ahasuerus repudiated his previous queen, Vashti, because of a misdemeanour. His household organise a beauty contest to find a replacement, and the choice falls on Esther. She is a Jewess, the niece and ward of Mordecai, a man-about-court, who at first seems to have no particular function, apart from being adviser to Esther. He tells her to keep quiet about her Jewish origins. This seems odd. How could a Jewess become Queen of a Persian court without the fact being noticed? It is true that the title of Queen does not seem to put her on a par with the King. She is more like a favourite concubine, who has to make a special request for any meeting that has not been initiated by him. And it so happens that the King's right-hand man is one Haman, who dislikes the Jews, and especially Mordecai, because Mordecai does not show him the respect he considers to be his due.

Actually, Esther's situation raises a broader issue, which is never properly resolved within the context of the Old Testament. Is it possible for a believing Jew, whether male or female, to "marry out"?

I remember reading somewhere that when F.R. Leavis married his wife, Queenie, her orthodox family had the prayers for the dead recited in her name. Yet in the Old Testament, Moses marries Zipporah, Solomon is united with the daughter of a Pharaoh, Boaz, as we shall see, marries Ruth, who was brought up in a different religion, and Mordecai does not protest when Esther becomes Queen to Ahasuerus; indeed, he seems rather to approve of the marriage. At the same time, two at least of the prophets, Ezra and Nehemiah, inveigh against mixed marriages. Ezra, in particular, who has a claim to be the most dislikeable of the prophets, has more than one unpleasant feature. He shows no compunction in accepting financial help from Artaxerxes, King of the Persians, towards the rebuilding of Jerusalem. (Artaxerxes no doubt wished to ingratiate with himself with the God of the Jews, who was said to be so powerful, although visibly capricious). But should a Jew accept non-Jewish gold in order to rebuild his sacred edifices? Ezra accepts the money without debating the issue, but later declares himself scandalised by the number of mixed marriages that have taken place during the captivity. He assembles the Israelites and calls upon the men who have taken foreign wives and produced half-foreign children, to admit that they have sinned against the Lord, and must repudiate both wives and children. This they agree to do with acclamation, and there is no mention in the text of any provision being made for the abandoned families. Readers who remember the Thirties will recall that a similar measure was applied in Nazi Germany, but with the Jews as victims. "Aryans" were obliged to divorce their Jewish wives, who mostly sought refuge abroad. A prophet, whose policy anticipates that of Nazi Germany, seems out of place in Holy Writ.[10]

---

[10] One of my war-time colleagues, who became a close family friend, was a non-orthodox Jewess, who had been forced into such an artificial divorce. She never saw her husband again; eventually she heard from her mother-in-law that he had been killed on the Russian front.

But to go back to Esther and Haman. The latter, who becomes increasingly hostile to the Jews, persuades Ahasuerus, a monarch apparently without any mind of his own, to publish an edict decreeing the persecution, and even killing, of all Israelites within the borders of the country. Mordecai appears at the palace gates in sackcloth and ashes to impress upon Esther that she must intercede with the king. Meanwhile, it has been accidentally discovered that Mordecai previously foiled a plot to murder the king, a good deed for which he has never been rewarded. Ahasuerus, suddenly apprised of this, becomes well disposed towards Mordecai, exactly at the point when Haman, with excessive confidence, is having a gallows built, on which to hang Mordecai. Esther decides to make her move. Like Judith, she decks herself in all her finery, but hers, of course is royal apparel. She requests the King to attend "a banquet of wine," at which only Haman and she will be the other people present. In the course of the meal, she pleads with the king to stop the persecution of the Jews. He appears not to read the edicts he signs, because he is incensed: "Who durst do this?", he asks[11], and rushes out into the garden to cool off. Haman, having been denounced, humbles himself before Esther to plead for his life. Ahasuerus, more and more ridiculous, assumes that Haman is trying to seduce the Queen under the royal nose in the royal palace. A court chamberlain puts an end to the farce by pointing out that a gallows is conveniently ready, and Haman is strung up on the gibbet he had prepared for Mordecai.

There is now a complete reversal of roles. Mordecai succeeds Haman as the most powerful man in the kingdom (cf. Joseph in

---

[11] Ahasuerus reminds me of an incident which occurred in the more prosaic setting of an annual Faculty meeting. An irascible colleague demanded to know who on earth had chaired the sub-committee responsible for the foolish motion about to be put to the vote. The administrative official, after consulting his files, replied, keeping an admirably straight face: "Yourself, Professor."

Egypt and Daniel also in Persia), and the Jews are given the right to take revenge on their enemies: –

... they slew of them that hated them seventy and five thousand; but on the spoil they laid not their hand.

This was done on the thirteenth day of the month of Adar; and on the fourteenth day of the same, they rested and made it a day of feasting and gladness (Est. 9.16, 17.)

And many from among the peoples of the land became Jews; for the fear of the Jews was fallen upon them. (Est. 8.17.)[12]

To stamp out the trouble root and branch, Esther requests that Haman's ten sons should be hanged like their father; request granted.[13] This is the origin of the Feast of Purim which is celebrated by orthodox Jews.

An unanswerable question lingers in the memory: *pace* Prophet

---

[12] This is one of the very rare mentions of conversion to Judaism; the motive is fear. I suspect a computer count would reveal that fear is one of the commonest words in the Old Testament.

[13] In making the request, Esther infringes the rule stated in Deut. 24.6: "... neither shall the children be put to death for the fathers."

As it happens, the book of Esther was adapted for stage performance by no less a person than the French tragedian, Jean Racine. *Esther* (1689) is subtitled tragédie, although it ends "happily" with the triumph of Esther and Mordecai, and belongs to the final, pious phase of Racine's career. It is a time-serving piece of flattery adapted to the circumstances of Louis XIV's court, and has no particular merit, apart from the smooth, accomplished flow of the verse. Mme de Maintenon commissioned it for performance by the impoverished daughters of aristocrats, whom she housed at the Collège de Saint-Cyr. It has a prologue presenting Louis XIV as God's most loyal servant on earth, and the scourge of heretics. There is a chorus or virtuous young Jewish girls, whom Esther is secretly educating in the Persian royal palace! Ahasuerus is so overburdened with his kingly duties that it escapes his notice that his Queen is Jewish, and that he has signed the anti-Jewish edict. Haman is an upstart and therefore a villain, and worst of all an Amalekite, whose forebears must somehow have escaped the massacre ordered by God. Since this is polite literature, no mention is made of the Jewish revenge, or of the hanging of Haman's ten sons.

Ezra, how many unacceptable Persian-Jewish children did Queen Esther have with the egregious Ahasuerus?

. . . .

We move on to the story of Ruth, a little pastoral tale, in which there are no killings and no unpleasant people, apart from God himself, who comes in for a little incidental criticism. The Bayard commentary describes it as "*un chef d'œuvre de la littérature biblique*"; "masterpiece" is perhaps an excessive term, but it stands out as the one book distinguished by some gentleness of feeling.

Following a recurrent pattern, there is again a famine in the Promised Land which, as it turned out, did not always flow with milk and honey. A Jewish woman, Naomi, with her husband, Elimelech and their two sons, seeks refuge in the land of Moab. Shortly afterwards, Elimelech dies. The sons marry Moabite women, Orpah and Ruth, but the sons too die after ten years, leaving Naomi alone with her daughters-in-law. Learning that the famine is over in Judah ("the Lord had visited his people and given them bread"), she decides to go home. She pleads with her daughters-in-law to go back to their mothers' houses, and to find new husbands ("it grieveth me much for your sakes, for the hand of the Lord has gone forth against me.") Orpah obeys, but Ruth insists on accompanying Naomi back to Judah ("thy people shall be my people, and thy God my God").

Once installed, Ruth goes gleaning in the barley fields to provide for their subsistence. Her beauty is noticed by Boaz, a wealthy farmer, who is an older man, and a kinsman of Elimelech, Naomi's dead husband. When Boaz learns who Ruth is, he instructs his servants to give her preferential treatment. Naomi, having noted Boaz's interest, turns matchmaker, and works out a strategy. Ruth must adorn and perfume herself (cf. Judith and Esther), and keep watch in the evening to see exactly where Boaz, having eaten and drunk his fill (cf.

the feast in *Judith*, and "the banquet of wine" in *Esther*), goes to sleep on the threshing floor. She must then steal up to him and "uncover his feet." I have already mentioned in connection with the Zipporah episode, that according to the commentaries, "feet" is a euphemism for "private parts." The Bayard Version says that Ruth *le découvrit* (uncovered him). The English Version continues "at midnight the man was afraid and turned himself: and behold a woman lay at his feet." The French says, *"au milieu de la nuit, Boaz frissonna"* (shivered, presumably because he was at least partly, if not entirely, naked), *"se tourna et vit une femme à son côté"* (turned over and saw a woman at his side). The English Ruth resorts to what seems to be another euphemism: "spread thy skirt over thine handmaiden, for thou art a near kinsman." The French Ruth goes straight to the point: *"Prends-moi pour femme, car tu es mon proche parent et mon défenseur."* (take me as thy wife, because thou art a near kinsman and my defender).

What she says relates to the rule that if a married man died without issue, it was the duty of his brother or his nearest kinsman to impregnate the widow, so as to "raise up seed" to the dead man. The commentaries do not explain how long the rule lasted, but certainly in the early days God was ruthless with someone who did not comply. This is another case of God "slaying" directly. When Onan (Gen. ch.38) deliberately "spilled his seed", God slew him, but the method is not specified. As for Boaz, the first gentleman we have so far come across in the Bible, apart perhaps from Joseph in his relationship with his brothers, he does not take advantage of the lady there and then. He explains to Ruth that she must hurry off home discreetly, because there is another kinsman with a prior claim; he will look into the matter on the morrow. The next day, he arranges a public confrontation with the other kinsman who, for reasons of his own, waives his right of priority. Boaz and Ruth can be happily united. Ruth promptly produces a son who, in the fullness of time,

51

will be the great-grandfather of King David.

Each of the female adventures is, then, a success story. All three heroines make legitimate use of their charms as a basic weapon. In addition, Judith, by a careful combination of ruse and piety, wins the trophy of the severed head, saves the town and earns everlasting fame. Esther, already a queen in a foreign court, uses her influence to defend her people, and sees her uncle become the right-hand man of the foreign king. This is either great success or a higher form of submission, depending on your viewpoint. Ruth begins as a gleaner in the fields, and then eventually becomes the wife of the landowner, although originally, her God was not the same as his God. And, despite being a Moabite, she contributes to the future royal Jewish line. The Bible is full of rules, but obviously admits of various compromises.

5

Some Moral Issues

The atmosphere of the Old Testament is so fraught with conflict, confusion and unhappiness that it seems legitimate to ask what moral lessons, if any, emerge from so much turmoil. However, in order to avoid misunderstanding, before I proceed further, I must emphasise that I am not presuming to comment on the Jewish religion as such. I know little about it, and am particularly ignorant of what it may have retained or discarded of the text of the Old Testament, as given in the English Bible. It is only with this text that I am concerned, as I encountered it, or as it was imposed upon me, within the context of a Christian education. My quarrel, in so far as I have one, is with those adults who assumed that, because the Old Testament was classed as part of Holy Writ, it was a suitable intellectual and emotional diet for the young, in its raw, unexplained form. Any child can see that there is a great deal in it which is not at all holy. And I may add that far from considering the New Testament spontaneously as a sequel to the Old, or as a renewal of the supposed covenant, as Prévost and Myre would have it, I felt the two parts of the Bible to be in flat contradiction with each other on many points. One was a closed system, the other open, and although I could no more espouse the New Testament than I could the Old, it did not evoke the same feeling of revulsion.

What was so sad about the Old Testament story, was that it did not seem to allow even a minimum of free will. A capricious God had the Jewish people on a leash; he led them this way and that, without fully justifying his decisions, and often without explaining why he was suddenly in a rage. He presented himself in two totally different guises: –

For the Lord thy God is a devouring fire, a jealous God. (*Deut.* 4, 24).

For the Lord thy God is a merciful God, he will not fail thee, neither destroy thee, nor forget the covenant of thy fathers, which he swore unto them. (*Deut.* 4, 31.)

The merciful God is not much in evidence anywhere in the text. Although, in *Deut.* 7, 14. , he makes the promise: "The Lord will take away all sickness," he is a willing spreader of pestilence, and chapter 28 of the same book gives a fearsome list of the maladies that will afflict any transgressor who opposes his will: –

The Lord shall smite thee with consumption, and with fever, and with inflammation, and with the fiery heat, and with the sword, and with blasting, and with a mildew; and they shall pursue thee until thou perish.

These dire threats continue for another twenty verses or more, and this is only one of the contexts in which God gives vent to his bile. We can only wonder at the mentality of the prophets who thought up the possibility of these terrible sufferings. At one point, the *Schadenfreude* is so strong that they make God cry neurotically that he *needs* to feel feared in order to curb his lust to punish: –

Oh that there were such heart in them that they would fear me and keep my commandments always, that it might be well with them and their children forever. (*Deut.* 5. 29.)

It is significant that the Ten Commandments, in which the main moral lesson may be thought to be enshrined, contain no expression of God's kindness to man. They are mainly prohibitions, preceded by the usual injunction that this God shall be feared, loved and obeyed "*before* all others." The tone is urgent enough to suggest that these other Gods might be actual rivals, so that "jealous," when applied to the Lord does not simply mean "pernickety as regards obedience," but may imply actual jealousy of other divine entities championing other nations. If this is so, the Old Testament is not monotheistic, as one is inclined at first to assume; the non-universality of the Jewish God may signify that the concept of absolute monotheism had not yet been attained. I shall argue later that Jesus represents true monotheism, despite the complexity introduced by the inventors of the so-called Trinity: the Father, the Son and the Holy Ghost, for which, as far as I can see, there is no authority in the bible itself.

. . . .

It is noticeable that the biblical text pays far more attention to the details of ritual than to the principles of moral behaviour. Much space is devoted to the rules governing the different animals prescribed for sacrifice, their species, their gender, their age and so on. The vestments of the priests are described in detail and so are their gestures in disposing of the blood from the animals.

Some points of civic virtue are clearly stated: "Thou shalt not kill," "Thou shalt not steal," "Thou shalt not covet thy neighbour's wife" etc., but they seem to be operative only within the tribal area; and even there rather uncertainly. After so many accounts of manslaughter, "Thou shalt not kill" rings rather hollow. That is the text in the Authorised Version; the Revised Version, embarrassed no doubt by the thought that God is contradicting himself, changes the wording to "Thou shalt not commit murder." A murder is a private killing for personal reasons, whereas God usually kills or causes to kill *en masse*, and in accordance with his divine will, whether overt or obscure. But here again things are not quite clear. As it happens, the most notorious murder in the Old Testament is Cain's killing of his brother, Abel, but God is implicated in it to some extent. He is not impartial in his attitude towards the two brothers; they are both industrious, and bring him tribute as required, but for some reason he prefers Abel and snubs Cain. Hence, Cain's jealousy.

. . . .

God's application of his moral laws is inconsistent in some other cases too. He attaches enormous importance to the Sabbath as a day of rest, when even servants were supposed to be relieved of work. One wonders why he is so dogmatic, because even the prophets must have known that in an agricultural community, there can be no complete break in the continuity of work. Milch cows need to be relieved of their burden of milk every day, if they are not to become uncomfortable. There is also the old adage: "Make hay while the sun shines," which must have had some relevance even for ancient Jewish agriculture. And animals, not recognising the days of the week, sometimes fall ill or give birth on Sundays, and have to be cared for. From the beginning, there must have been all sorts of compromises in order to circumvent this purely ritualistic rule, which runs counter to everyday living. The height of absurdity is reached in *Numbers*, 15, 32 where a man is discovered gathering sticks in the wilderness on the Sabbath. Moses consults the Lord about the appropriate sanction; the Lord replies: "The man must surely be stoned to death," and the sentence is duly carried out. Moses seem to take this episode in his stride, but imagine the consternation of Good King Wenceslas, faced with such an executive decision, and remembering the precedent of *Numbers* 15, 32: –

> Oh dear! Yonder peasant has obviously forgotten that this year the Feast of Stephen falls on a Sabbath. There he goes, thoughtlessly gathering winter fuel, instead of piously succumbing to hypothermia. I suppose I must arrange for him

to be stoned to death. How upsetting, and in the festive season too!

King David, on the other hand, breaks a major rule. Not only does he covet Bathsheba, the wife of his subordinate Uriah; he has Uriah put in the front line of battle so that his death is certain, leaving David free to marry Bathsheba. The Lord is "displeased" about this, and sends the prophet Nathan to David to lecture to him by means of a parable about the rich man being unfair to the poor man. Before David realises that the parable is referring to himself, he exclaims indignantly that the rich man should be put to death. However, he escapes this fate. God punishes him by causing the death of the first child he has with Bathsheba. But the second child survives to become eventually King Solomon "in all his glory." One law for the Lord's anointed, another for the gatherers of sticks.

Did Solomon ever know that his father had commissioned the killing of his mother's first husband? The biblical text does not say. But if he knew, he was not the sort of man to waste time on Hamlet-like self-questioning. Once he was anointed king through court intrigue and with the support of Nathan, the emissary of the Lord, he had his possible rivals quickly eliminated. "Thou shalt not kill" – but *raison d'état* may provide a sufficient dispensation. It should be noted that this moral dubiety occurs within the Chosen People, and with the tacit or supposed consent of the Lord.

6

The Four Books of Complaint

The ambiguity of God's behaviour towards his Chosen People, and the uncertainty of the moral lessons to be deduced from that behaviour, are revealed most extensively in what one might call the Four Books of Complaint: *The Psalms, Lamentations, Job* and *Ecclesiastes.* The Psalms and Lamentations are linked to some extent to the Babylonian exile; Job and Ecclesiastes are unconnected with any specific historical incident. In the English canon, Job, the Psalms, and Ecclesiastes are close together, but Lamentations is placed much further on, after five other books, two of which – Isaiah and Jeremiah – are very long, and consist of the usual mixture of objurgations and threats on the part of the prophets or God himself with occasional professions of submission on the part of the Chosen People. Such texts can make wearisome reading because, as I have already said, it is often impossible to tell exactly what God or the prophets are incensed about, since they express themselves in such general and repetitive terms. I shall need to return to Isaiah later.

However, in the four texts I have singled out as constituting a sort of biblical Wailing Wall, it is not so much a question of God or the prophets berating the people, as of certain individuals doubting the benevolence of God's providence.

Let us consider first the Psalms. Jean-Pierre Prévost in his general introduction to the Old Testament, refers to them in laudatory terms: –

... ce recueil de poèmes, chants, prières qui compte parmi les œuvres les plus universellement appréciées de la Bible...

(this collection of poems, songs and prayers which is one of the most universally appreciated sections of the Bible.)

"Universally" is open to question. Marc Sevin, a translator who provides the particular introduction to the Psalms does not discuss their content, but concentrates entirely on the complexities of their prosody in the original Hebrew, which make them difficult to render adequately in a modern language. However, I doubt whether even in the original language, the prosodic complexities can conceal the fact that the themes running through the 150 Psalms are limited, monotonous and contradictory. Taken as a sort of sonnet sequence, the psalms are very uneven.

The general ground-note is sounded in the phrase "The fear of the Lord is the beginning of wisdom" (111, 10.). The religion of the Psalms is based on acute anxiety. God is all-powerful, difficult to obey, because his intentions and preferences are not always clear, and quick to anger. He must be kept appeased by a constant chorus of praise: –

Praise ye the Lord. Blessed is the man that feareth the Lord (112, 1.).

Praise ye the Lord – Blessed be the name of the Lord from this time forth and forever (113, 1, 2.).

These, or similar phrases, occur innumerable times, and become so automatic as to lose any poetic force. The fear is sometimes tempered by a provisional declaration of confidence in God's care for his Chosen People, and his hatred of all the nations beyond the pale[14]: –

---

14 There are very occasional references to the Lord's possible universality for all nations. But this universality is not spontaneous on God's side. The nations will *(cont. overleaf)*

The Lord is on my side; I will not fear: what can man do unto
me? (118, 6.)

The confidence may remain complete for the duration of some short
psalm, as in 121, which, in the Authorised Version, begins with the
haunting line: –

I will lift up mine eyes to the hills, from whence cometh my help ...

Similarly confident is No 23, an affirmation of God's total
benevolence, and a harmonious expression of a yearning for
happiness, based on the dubious pastoral symbol of the shepherd: –

The Lord is my shepherd; I shall not want ...

But even here a shadow is cast by the strange expression: "Thou
preparest a table before me in the presence of mine enemies." Who,
apart from some vengeful, gloating person, could enjoy, and happily
digest, a meal eaten with enemies looking on? And how, if enemies
are present – and they crop up everywhere in the Psalms, without
their identity or the causes of their hostility ever being made explicit
– can the psalmist relax enough to assert?: –

Surely goodness and mercy shall follow me all the days of my
life, and I shall live in the house of the Lord forever.

At school, Psalm No 23, was the only one we were required to learn
by heart; there was no mention of No 22, which expresses the
opposite mood: –

My God, my God, why hast thou foresaken me? Why art thou
so far from helping me ... ?

Through all five books of the Psalms, passionate complaints of this
kind alternate with declarations of praise, frequently within the same
psalm, as if, having dared to voice his dissatisfaction with God's
behaviour, the psalmist took fright and launched into another torrent
of fulsome worship, which is meant to serve as an insurance. It is true

---

come to him, since they will recognise him as being the most powerful God. There will be
a dominant element of fear in their conversion.

that, very occasionally, thanks are rendered for benefits received, and it is taken for granted that they come directly from God and are not an effect of chance. More often, the reproaches come thick and fast, and the symbol of the protective shepherd[15] is completely exploded (Psalm 44): –

In God have we made our boast all day long, and we will give thanks unto thy name forever. But now thou hast cast us off, and brought us to dishonour, and goest not for forth with our host. Thou hast given us like sheep appointed for meat, and hast scattered us among the nations.

---

[15] Since I spent part of my early childhood in a farming area, I have always known that shepherds are not sentimental about their charges. It is the sheep-farmer's wife and his children who cherish the orphaned pet lamb. But eventually it too becomes a sheep, and goes the way of all sheep flesh, leaving only a faint memory. Besides, next year, there will probably be another orphaned pet lamb. The point is expressed by the poet André Chénier (1762-94) in a few perfect lines, which he wrote in prison while waiting to be summoned to the guillotine. He is referring, of course, to his own imminent sad end: –

Quand, au mouton bêlant la sombre boucherie
Ouvre ses cavernes de mort,
Pâtres, chiens et moutons, toute la bergerie
Ne s'informe plus de son sort.
Les enfants qui suivaient ses ébats dans la plaine,
Les vierges aux belles couleurs
Qui le baisaient en foule et sur sa blanche laine
Entrelaçaient rubans et fleurs,
Sans plus penser à lui le mangent s'il est tendre.

(When, to the bleating sheep, the sombre slaughter-house
Opens its caves of death,
Shepherds, dogs, fellow sheep, all of them,
Take no further interest in his fate.
The children who followed his frolickings in the pasture,
The rosy-cheeked girls
Who crowded around to kiss him, and in his white fleece
Entwined ribbons and flowers,
Without giving him another thought, eat him if he is tender.)

All this has come upon us: yet have we not forgotten thee, neither have we dealt falsely in thy covenant.

Yea, for thy sake are we killed all the day long; and we are counted as sheep for the slaughter.

Awake, why sleepest thou, Lord? arise, cast us not off forever.

Wherefore hidest thou thy face, and forgettest our afflictions and our oppression?

How fallacious, then, are the serene assurances of Psalm 23: –

He maketh me to lie down in green pastures: he leadeth me beside the still waters.

He restoreth my soul.

. . . .

Lamentations also blows hot and cold, in the sense that, like the Psalms, it makes some faint attempts to justify the ways of God to his Chosen People, and then lapses into bitter despair: –

The Lord is righteous: for I have rebelled against his commandments: hear, I pray, all ye peoples, and behold my sorrow ... (Lam. 1, 15).

Behold, O Lord; for I am in distress; my bowels are troubled; mine heart is turned within me; for I have grievously rebelled: abroad the sword bereaveth, at home there is as death (Lam. 1, 20).

After this rather apologetic introduction, Chapter 3 suddenly pours out a litany of reproachful metaphors: –

I am the man that hath seen affliction by the rod of his wrath.

He hath led me and caused me to walk in darkness and not in light.

Surely against me he turneth his hand again and again all the day.

My flesh and my skin has he made old; he hath broken my

bones.

He hath builded against me, and compassed me with gall and travail.

He hath made me dwell in dark places, as those that have long been dead.

He hath filled me with bitterness, he hath sated me with wormwood. (Lam. 3, 1-15).

There is a short lull during which the speaker, once again, tries to persuade himself that the "casting off" by God will not be permanent: –

For though he cause grief, yet will he have compassion according to the multitude of his mercies.

For he does not afflict willingly, nor grieve the children of men.

Let us search and try our ways, and turn again to the Lord. (Lam. 3, 33-40).

"Search and try our ways" clearly implies that the sufferers are puzzled about what they may have done wrong. Then the litany of complaints resumes during the rest of Chapter 3, continues during Chapter 4, and closes the book in Chapter 5 on a completely negative note: –

Wherefore dost thou forget us forever, and forsake us so long time?

Turn thou us unto thee, O Lord, and we shall be turned; renew our days of old.

But thou hast utterly rejected us, thou art very wroth against us. (Lam. 5, 20 -22).

. . . .

Job and *Ecclesiastes* are the strangest books in the Old Testament because, in their different ways, they come close to subverting all the rest. Job contains the fiercest, sustained attack on the concept of God the protective shepherd of his flock, God the merciful, God the champion of the virtuous and the scourge of the wicked. At the same time, it is wildly incoherent, as if it had been written by at least two different authors pulling in different directions, and the tone oscillates between the sublime and the ridiculous. Some of the verses are among the most poetic and memorable in the whole of the Bible, yet certain details of the story are frankly vulgar.

At the beginning, Satan makes one of his rare appearances, but we are left to wonder about his status. He attends a meeting of "the sons of God," a celestial assembly not previously mentioned. The plural puts the future of Jesus in doubt as "the only begotten son," unless we take "begotten" to mean "incarnate," whereas these other sons, whoever they are, exist only as spirits. Satan obviously has a right to attend the meeting in the presence of the Lord – there is no question here of "Get thee behind me, Satan!" – but is he a full member? Is he a son? We are not told, but he and the Lord are on speaking terms, because the Lord, making polite conversation as any Royal personage is supposed to do, asks: "Whence comest thou?" Satan answers with the all-embracing statement: "from going to and fro in the earth, and from walking up and down in it."[16] The atmosphere is convivial, so much so that the Lord boasts about his "servant" Job in the land of Uz, a perfect, upright, God-fearing man, and Satan comments cheekily that Job is only perfect because God has showered benefits upon him – he is a wealthy man and he is blessed with seven sons and three daughters. Put him to the test, says Satan, and he will crack. Thereupon, the two supernatural entities, like two men arguing in a pub, have a bet with each other. Let Satan do his worst, short of endangering Job's life, and we shall see what happens. This is the first vulgarity: the Lord, who has so often proclaimed that he will defend

---

[16] Satan is obviously not resident in Hell, and indeed it is difficult to tell at what point Hell and Hell-fire came into existence. There is no Hell as such in the Old Testament, only Sheol or "the pit," where the dead are dead once and for all.

the righteous, gives Satan a free hand in the most careless and flippant way. Satan acts promptly. He wipes out Job's wealth, and sends a wind which kills his seven sons (the fate of the daughters is not mentioned). Job accepts this first blow with resignation: –

... the Lord gave and the Lord taketh away;

Blessed be the name of the Lord. (1.21).

A little later, the Lord and Satan have another convivial meeting, at which, in effect, the Lord says to Satan: "Have another go!" This time, Satan infects Job with boils "from the sole of his foot unto his crown"; Job's wife urges him to give up his belief in God, but he chides her: –

What? shall we receive good at the hand of God, and shall we not receive evil?

This again is an expression of resignation, but it includes the admission that God is capable of sending evil for his own inscrutable purposes.

At this point, Job is visited by three "friends," Eliphaz, Bildad and Zophar, who come to console him. After seven days and seven nights of silence, Job's nerve breaks, and he bewails his lot in the most pathetic terms: –

Let the day perish wherein I was born, and the night which said, there is a man-child conceived.

Why did I not die from the womb? Why did I not give up the ghost when I came out of the belly?

I am not at ease, neither am I quiet, neither have I rest: but trouble cometh. (Job. 3).

Eliphaz is the first of the visitors to raise his voice in consolation, although the term is hardly appropriate. It must be said that Job is unlucky in his "friends." All three are pompous to the point of comedy, and repeat irrelevant commonplaces, as if they were incapable of understanding what Job is talking about. Eliphaz asserts that the innocent never perish (but what about the seven sons who have just been wiped out?), and that God's justice is mysterious.

Eliphaz has had his own little revelation, which he describes self-importantly: –

Now a thing was secretly brought to me, and mine ear received a whisper thereof.

In thoughts from visions of the night, when deep sleep falleth upon men.

Then a spirit passed before my face; the hair of my flesh stood up.

… and I heard a voice saying

Shall mortal man be more just than God? shall a man be more just than his Maker? (Job. 4, 12-17).

Eliphaz prates on throughout Chapter 5, saying complacently: "Behold, happy is the man whom God correcteth: therefore despise not thou the chastening of the Almighty," and asserts gratuitously that everything will end happily.

But Job is not mollified. He insists that he has a right to protest: –

Therefore I will not refrain my mouth; I will speak in the anguish of my spirit; I will complain in the bitterness of my soul (7, 11).

He is indignant because he has not been told what he has done wrong. As we know from the beginning of the story, he has done nothing wrong. He is the innocent victim of a bet between God and Satan. His fate corresponds exactly to the pagan lament that Shakespeare puts into the mouth of Lear: –

As flies to wanton boys are we to the Gods,

They kill us for their sport.

The Lord and Satan are even more cruel than the pagan gods, because instead of killing him outright, they prolong his suffering.

If I have sinned, what do I do unto thee, O thou watcher of men? Why hast thou set me as a mark for thee, so that I am a burden to myself? (7, 20).

It is now Bildad's turn to indulge in the same pious commonplaces as

Eliphaz. It is impossible that God should be unjust. We know this through tradition; it is a lesson we learned from our fathers: –

For we are but of yesterday, and know nothing, because our days upon the earth are but a shadow. (8, 9).

Even so, he is sure that everything will turn out to be for the best: –

He (God) will yet fill thy mouth with laughter, and thy lips with shouting. (8, 9).

Job now weakens slightly, and agrees that man cannot be on a par with God, but he does not lose hold of his central point. For a moment, he generalises the problem. Evil triumphs everywhere; who allows this? "If it not be *he* (God), who then is it?" (9, 24). Then he reverts to his particular pain, and reasserts his need for an explanation: –

My soul is weary with my life; I will give free course to my complaint: I will speak in the bitterness of my soul.

I will say unto God. Do not condemn me; show me wherefore thou contendest with me. (10, 12).

The third friend, Zophar, now weighs in with a far from soothing suggestion. Since Job is being made to suffer, he must be guilty, although he is unaware of any guilt. But who can penetrate the wisdom of God?: –

Canst thou by searching find out God? Canst thou find out the Almighty unto perfection? (11, 7).

Job, he implies, is only a man: –

But vain man is void of understanding, yea man is born as a wild ass's colt. (11, 12).

But let him hope, and he will surely "lift up his face without a spot." (11, 15).

Job jibs at this: –

But I have understanding as well as you: I am not inferior to you; yea, who knoweth not such things as these? (12, 3).

In other words, keep quiet if you have nothing original to say. Job persists in his attitude of protest: –

Surely, I would speak with the Almighty and I desire to reason with God.

Though he slay me, yet will I wait for him: nevertheless I will maintain my ways before him.

Behold now, I have ordered my cause;

I know that I am righteous.

Wilt thou harass a driven leaf? And wilt thou pursue the dry stubble?

Job again generalises his predicament: –

Man that is born of a woman is of few days, and full of trouble.

He cometh forth like a flower, and is cut down: he fleeth also as a shadow and continueth not. (14. 1, 1).

Man is transient, but while he is still alive

… his flesh upon him hath pain, and his soul within him mourneth. (14. 22).

Eliphaz, still the stern, uncomprehending "friend," accuses Job of empty, sacrilegious talk: –

Should a wise man make answer with vain knowledge, and fill his belly with the east wind? (15. 2).

His own belly is full of wind, because he amplifies at length the gratuitous assertion that God will inevitably punish the wicked.

Job, justifiably exasperated, angrily exclaims, "Miserable comforters are ye all!", and fills chapters 16 and 17 with a further account of his sufferings.

While Job pauses for breath, Bildad takes up the theme of the inevitable sufferings of the wicked, with a wealth of metaphors about nets, nooses, gins and traps. He is still oblivious to the fact that the subject of the debate is not the wished-for sufferings of the wicked, but the apparently unfair sufferings of the righteous. Job becomes impatient, as well he might:–

How long will you yet vex my soul, and break me in pieces with words? (19.2).

But the argument drags on, without progressing, for a few more chapters, during which Eliphaz and Bildad prosily repeat themselves, and Job for a while joins in the chorus of denunciations of the wicked. Occasionally, for the first time, he too seems to forget the main thread of his discourse[17] but eventually he returns to the central dilemma: why does God ill-treat the righteous who try to obey him?

Then suddenly, without warning and out of nowhere, there emerges a brash young popinjay called Elihu, who presumes to announce his disagreement with what has been said so far. However, he cannot have been listening very attentively, because he proceeds to repeat at length the argument already put forward by the trio of non-comforters: the Almighty, being Lord of the universe, is above human justice. Elihu is as self-important as Eliphaz – "I have yet somewhat to say on God's behalf" – and he fills chapters 32 to 37 with his superfluous chatter.

At length, he is interrupted by no less a person than the Lord himself, who arrives impressively in a whirlwind. Does he, as you might expect, say to Job, "Not to worry. It was only a little wager between myself and my old acquaintance, Satan. Apologies for any inconvenience caused." He does not; in fact, as a dear old friend of ours used to say when in her emphatic mood: "I can't begin to tell you how absolutely not!" God does not mention Satan. Instead, he adopts a device, for which there is a good French expression: *il noie le poisson*, he drowns the fish, that is, he swamps the central issue in a deluge of irrelevant details. He launches into a grandiose catalogue of the marvels of the universe and keeps asking Job can he, Job, do this, or that. "Will the wild ass be content to serve thee? ... Canst thou draw out leviathan with a fish-hook?", etc. Obviously, Job

---

[17] It is he, for instance, who says unexpectedly: "I know that my redeemer liveth." I shall return to this point later. It is both mysterious and important.

cannot out-bully God, so he caves in: "I am of small account ... I will proceed no further." (Ch. 40). So the argument fizzles out inconclusively, although from the rational point of view, Job has won a clear moral victory. God is a hypocrite, and he has avoided the nub of the question. The supposed covenant between God and man makes no sense at all, if man is expected to keep to its terms and God is free to flout them.

The end of the book is a shambles. God, like Elihu, cannot have been listening properly either, because he now inexplicably finds fault with the trio of cold-comforters, who have been defending his cause all along. They must do penance on Job's behalf by offering up seven bullocks and seven rams, a completely irrelevant procedure in this context.

There is a final touch of vulgarity. God restores Job's wealth, which is even greater than before, and again supplies him with seven sons and three daughters, although it is not clear whether this is a new brood, or the previous children miraculously resuscitated. God seems to work on the dubious principle that the evil he has caused may be expunged without trace. That may be true for God; it is not so true for man.

The thought occurs that Handel's genius, through the absence of a cynical collaborator to write the libretto, may have missed an opportunity here. The Book of Job might be turned into a fascinating tragi-comic oratorio. It could begin with the wager duet between God and Satan, two rival basso profundos, followed by a plangent solo from the baritone, Job; then interchanges between Job and the three "friends," in different comic registers to contrast with the fatuous flutings of the counter-tenor, Elihu. God could make a dramatic return as the *deus ex machina* to silence Job's complaints, and the piece could end with a mute, perplexed Job listening to a chorus of the five others, led by God himself, all singing lustily off the point and in God's praise. But perhaps the subject calls for the impishness of Rossini or Offenbach, or even Gilbert and Sullivan.

. . . .

Unlike the Book of Job, which tells a story and has a plot of sorts, Ecclesiastes makes no pretence of coherence. Like the Book of Proverbs itself, it is a collection of aphorisms and quasi-proverbs, odd or random sayings and lyrical outbursts. The Hebrew title is "The Words of Quohelet, the son of King David in Jerusalem," but the commentators seem to agree that this ascription to Solomon is a literary fiction adopted by the unknown author, whose words were recorded, or edited, by a disciple. Quohelet means "the Preacher," but the characteristic of this preacher is that his sermon exhibits a mixture of different philosophical attitudes, which he presents more or less on the same level. Consequently, he is much more modern in tone than any of the prophets, who keep hammering away monotonously at the stormy relationship between the Lord and the chosen People. Also, unlike Job, he is not concerned with the personal quandary of his grievance against God. He stands further back and, looking at life as a whole, he keeps repeating the phrase: "Vanity of vanities, all is vanity."

Within the context of the Old Testament, this is a profoundly sacrilegious statement. If life on earth, and particularly human life, is insignificant, this insignificance redounds on the Creator, who evaporates as a source of interest, and cannot be evoked as a guarantor of morality. The Preacher is anticipating the attitude of latter-day Nihilists. Or we can see a parallel with Hamlet's complaint: "How weary, stale, flat and unprofitable seem to me all the uses of this world." But Hamlet is generalising on the basis of his particular dilemma: his uncle has murdered his father, married his mother and usurped the throne. The Preacher is in no such pickle. He claims to have enjoyed all the advantages of kingship himself, but to have found them wanting. Vanity of vanities, all is vanity.

But since this is the Old Testament, he cannot quite overcome the fear of God, in which the volume is steeped. Every now and again, he introduces a cautionary clause so as to be on the safe side.

To the man that pleaseth him God giveth wisdom and knowledge. (2.26).

God shall judge. (3.12).

All the work of God is beyond comprehension. (8.17).

Fear God and keep his commandments. (11.10).

However, this Preacher is no ascetic; he is full-blooded; cheerfulness keeps breaking in, sometimes with a quite Falstaffian vigour, and even with the approval of a surprisingly benign God, who seems rather different from the hard taskmaster of the Chosen People: –

He hath made everything beautiful in its time; also he hath set the world in their heart … (3.11).

… a man hath no better thing under the sun, than to eat and drink and to be merry. (8.15).

Live joyfully with the wife thou lovest, all the days of thy life of vanity, which he (God) hath given thee under the sun; for that is thy portion in life. (9.19).

He is even cynical, and one can imagine the serious prophets frowning at him, and wondering how on earth he found his way into Holy Writ beside them: –

A feast is made for laughter, and wine maketh glad the life: and money answereth all things. (10.19).

Be not righteous over much; neither make thyself over wise; why should thou destroy thyself? (7.16).

Sometimes, he seems to talk deliberate nonsense just for fun, like Hamlet saying: "I am mad but north-north-west; when the wind is southerly, I know a hawk from a handsaw." For instance, what are we to make of the following maxims?

He that diggeth a pit shall fall into it; and whoso breaketh through a fence, a serpent shall bite him. (10.18).

If the serpent bite before it be charmed, then there is no advantage in the charmer. (10.10).

Cast thy bread upon the waters: for thou shall find it after many days. (11.1)[18]

Then again, there may be method in his inconsequentiality: –

Curse not the king, no, not in thy thought; and curse not the rich in thy bedchamber; for a bird of the air shall carry the voice, and that which hath wings shall tell the matter. (10.20).

. . . .

There is an oft-quoted sequence of verses, which at first seems to make sense, but which, on further examination, raises philosophical doubts. This is the series at the beginning of chapter 3: –

To everything there is a reason, and a time to every purpose under the heaven:

A time to be born, and a time to die; a time to plant, and a time to pluck up that which has been planted:

A time to kill and a time to heal; a time to break down, and a time to build up, etc.

The litany is obviously based on the annual cycle, or other regular cycles, in the animal and vegetable kingdoms. It is reassuring, since it implies that everything takes place in due course and at the appropriate moment, and is, therefore, in a way *necessary*. But the concept of necessity runs counter to the concept of vanity, in the

---

18 Commentators have pondered on this sodden offering to the self, which seems to be the structuralist opposite of a burnt offering to the Lord. One exegete suggests that it is a recommendation to the disciple to go into the maritime business! Another explains that you will eventually eat the fish which will have eaten your bread. This outcome would require a remarkable sequence of coincidences, and in any case how could you know that your bread had been eaten by this particular fish?

sense of pointlessness. Can things be at the same time necessary and pointless?

From one point of view, no. If the Preacher is suggesting that events in the human world are, like the seasons, subject to a meaningful rhythm (although even the meteorological rhythm, as we know, displays unexpected variations from year to year), he is contradicting himself. People are often born and often die at inappropriate moments, that is, "out of season" in relation to their particular context. The Preacher himself says: –

I returned and saw under the sun that the race is not to the swift, nor the battle to the strong, neither yet bread to the wise, nor riches to the men of understanding, nor yet favour to men of skill; *but time and chance happeneth to them all.*

For the first part of the sentence to be in harmony with the end, he should have said that the race is *not always* to the swift because, in the last resort, *chance* governs everything. This is a direct refutation of the idea, axiomatic in the rest of the Old Testament, that the Lord – "Oh thou watcher of men," as Job calls him in a phrase with sinister overtones – is personally supervising the doings on earth. If he is not, and everything is subject to chance, we have to fall back on the pagan concept of Fate that I mentioned earlier – the unknown, unknowable, impersonal force, the ultimate God behind all the limited, personal gods invented by man, whether they be Golden Calves or other mute idols, or imaginary voices speaking from bushes, clouds or whirlwinds. If we are tired of the tantrums of the God of the Old Testament, we can sigh with relief "Thank God!", but the entity we are thanking is not the phoney God in the foreground, but the unimaginable entity beyond our ken, for which our thanks or blame are presumably irrelevant. But we are left facing a conundrum; why did this impersonal entity create us as persons, while denying us the ability to be at rest in our non-knowing? That is the valid point behind the Book of Job, clumsily symbolised by the wager between the opposite figures of a limited god and an active devil.

The repetition of the phrase "Vanity of vanities, all is vanity" raises another problem. Why, if everything is pointless, does the Preacher bother to write a book to be entrusted to his disciple?

And furthermore, my son, be admonished: of making many books there is no end; and much study is a weariness of the flesh. (12.12).

The reason must be that he feels an urge to leave a record, to get the matter off his chest. He is using language to perpetuate his thought for as long as possible; its duration may not be eternal but, although he could not foresee this, it has already lasted some thousands of years, despite its many obscurities, or because of them, since they lend themselves to endless comment. "All is vanity" is an absolute truth only *sub specie aeternitatis*. Shelley states that broad truth perfectly in *Ozymandias*. But while we are engaged as individuals or groups in the process of living, we have to create temporary, provisional absolutes so as to give a focus to our activities, and thus it is that the concept of necessity reappears within the context of "all is vanity." The moral problem is how to ensure that the provisional absolutes are not harmful. The Preacher, bless him, nearly comes out into the clear as an Existentialist Absurdist.

. . . .

Nearly, but not quite, because towards the end of the book he gets into a muddle again between the alternatives of enjoying life for what it is worth while it is being lived, and fearing some ultimate judgement that the Creator is bound to enact: –

Rejoice, O young man, in thy youth; and let thy heart cheer thee in the days of thy youth, and walk in the ways of thine heart, and in the sight of thine eyes: but know thou, that for all these things God will bring thee into judgement.

This is gratuitous assertion, an echo of the belief in the unsatisfactory, limited, jealous, personal God, that the Preacher seemed to have transcended for a moment, when he glimpsed the possibility of a more mysterious Creative force above such partisan considerations, and expressing itself as fate. Only such a force, I repeat is consonant with the expression "all is vanity," since it effects a compromise between ultimate pointlessness and immediate necessity.

Ecclesiastes ends with what is perhaps the strangest of all biblical texts, verses 2 to 7 of chapter 12, beginning "Or ever the sun or the light and the moon and the stars be darkened ...," a sequence of images and metaphors which when read aloud have a powerful effect, but the details of which are completely indecipherable. It is a perfect example of the phatic beyond the reach of understanding; nobody knows the relevance of the "grasshopper shall be a burden, and the caper-berry shall fail," or of "the silver chord be loosed or the golden bowl be broken." I sense it to be a trance-like vision of the end of the world, when the ordinary sights and sounds of activity will cease, and the flame of life will be reabsorbed into its original, unimaginable source, leaving only a residue of inanimate dust. But that is only my subjective impression. I last heard the passage being read aloud during the television broadcast of the Queen Mother's funeral, and I was struck by the contrast between this uncanny hermetic incantation and the bouncy, avuncular, reassuringness of the Archbishop's discourse.

The Bayard Bible makes no attempt at an interpretation of the passage, but the *Bible de Jérusalem* adds further complexities by pointing out uncertainties in the translation of the images, and then makes a very surprising comment on the book as a whole: –

Le livre se termine comme il avait commencé, mais on mesure le chemin parcouru. Il a appris à l'homme sa misère, mais aussi sa grandeur, en lui montrant que ce monde n'est pas digne de lui. Il le provoque à une religion désintéressée, à une prière qui soit l'adoration de la créature consciente de son néant en présence du

mystère de Dieu.
(The book ends as it began, but one can see the ground that has been covered. It has revealed his wretchedness to man, but also his greatness, by showing him that this world is not worthy of him. It steers him towards a disinterested religion, a form of prayer, which is the adoration of the creature conscious of his nothingness in the presence of the mystery of God.)
Well, maybe, although I do not feel that adoration is by any means the keynote of the text. Its contradictions suggest rather a tension between the flesh and the faculty of reason. But what astonishes me most is the assertion, from a Catholic source, that this world is not worthy of man. It reminds me of a hymn, probably Nonconformist, the first words of which linger in my memory: "I'm but a stranger here, Heaven is my home." I always thought it presumptuous and unsingable; "Off with you then to Heaven. Misery Guts!" was my instinctive, rude response.

Is it not a strange notion to suppose that the anonymous, unknown creative power should have put us into a wrong world? Who are we to say that it is unworthy of us? This is the only world we know, and we have to try to come to terms with it. Is it not rather the case that the limited, personal God of the Old Testament, a God who needs to be feared and fed on a diet of praise, is grotesquely inadequate in the role of Creator? The fear of God, far from being the beginning of wisdom, is the origin of sinister superstitions.

7

A Mysterious Rhapsody

The Song of Songs is just as unexpected a book to find in the Old Testament as Ecclesiastes, and apparently its canonical status has given rise to similar differences of opinion over the centuries. It stands out because of several curious features. To begin with, it is the only book to contain one single, and moreover only oblique reference to God: –

> … love is as strong as death; jealousy is as cruel as the grave; its flashes are flashes of fire, the very flame of the Lord. (8, 6).

The reference is negative, since even in this amorous context, it associates God with jealousy, not with love. Next, to the ordinary reader, the Song must appear as an outburst of very human sexual passion, with no religious connection whatever, and no worthy purpose, such as the founding of a family or a dynasty, which is the normal, official justification for the unleashing of the anarchic sexual urge. It seems to be a pure expression of love for love's sake. The outburst is so fierce that it comes in sporadic jets, often of uncertain meaning in themselves, and without any obvious link connecting them. In fact, the text ranks as the most hermetic in the whole of the Bible, which, as we have seen, is not lacking in puzzles and obscurities. The commentaries in the Bayard Version and the Bible of

Jerusalem coincide only in eliminating certain initial confusions. The ascription of the work to Solomon is fictitious, like that of Ecclesiastes; the suggestion that it may have some connection with Solomon and the Queen of Sheba is untenable. There is no compelling reason to suppose that it may be an allegory symbolizing the relationship between the soul and God or between Christ (not yet born!) and his church. It is to be taken as a poem about human passion, but those who want to see more in it than that are free to do so, given the fact that the meaning is so elusive.

The two commentaries divide up the text differently. The Bible of Jerusalem sees it as five separate poems, plus an epilogue; Chapter 8, including "we have a little sister who hath no breasts," can be disregarded as a fragment from a quite different story, which may have found its way in by accident. The Bayard Version interprets the whole text as an exchange between a feminine and a masculine voice, with the feminine voice dominating, – an exchange in which other voices intervene haphazardly from time to time. The Bayard Version also asserts: –

Il est possible d'y trouver une cohérence à condition d'admettre qu'elle ne se réduit pas à une trame narrative linéaire.

(It is possible to see a coherent pattern in the text, provide we accept that it cannot be reduced to a linear, narrative sequence.)

Since this coherent pattern remains undemonstrated, we have to fall back on our own guesswork. There is certainly a pair of lovers, who praise each other's physical attributes with the most lush comparisons: –

… thine eyes are as doves behind thy veil, thy hair is as a flock of goats that lie along the side of mount Gilead…

Thy two breasts are like two fawns of a roe, which feed among the lilies…

Thou art all fair, my love: there is no spot in thee. (4, 1-5).

My beloved is white and ruddy, the chiefest among ten

thousand...

His cheeks are a bed of spices, as banks of sweet herbs; his lips are as lilies, dropping liquid myrrh.

His mouth is most sweet: yea, he is altogether lovely... (5, 10-16).

This is a pastoral idyll involving two people, but some of the verses contain incomprehensible references to other persons, e.g. –

Draw me: we will run after thee: the king hath brought me into his chambers: we will be glad and rejoice in thee, we will make mention of thy love more than of wine; rightly do they love thee. (1, 4).

On one occasion, exceptionally, the verses follow each other like a question and its answer: –

Tell me, O thou whom my soul loveth, where thou feedest thy flock, where thou makest it to rest at noon? For why should I be as one that is veiled beside the flocks of thy companions? (1, 5).

Here, the suggestion is that their love is being kept secret, and she is protesting about this. He gives an encouraging reply: follow us: –

If thou knowest not, O thou fairest among women, go thy way forth by the footsteps of the flock, and feed thy kids besides the shepherds' tents.

The mention of kids seems to define her as a goatherd, which makes it all the more difficult to believe that the sudden reference to "the king" in verse 12 is to be taken literally: –

While the king sat at his table, my spikenard sent forth its fragrance.

Perhaps we have to understand that while the young shepherd is eating his midday meal, the female feramones produce their effect, and the couple's love is consummated in the *al fresco* setting.

Behold thou art fair, my love; behold, thou art fair, thine eyes are as doves.

Behold, thou art fair, my beloved, yea pleasant: also our couch is green.

The beams of our house are cedars and our rafters are firs. (1, 15, 16, 17).

So, with a little imagination, one can turn these lyrical hints into a pleasing *après-midi d'un faune*.

But is it an inter-racial love affair? The voice in verse 5 was definitely female: –

I am black, but comely, O ye daughters of Jerusalem...

Look not upon me, because I am swarthy, because the sun has scorched me. My mother's sons were incensed against me, they made me keeper of the vineyards; but mine own vineyard have I not kept.

Is "black" to be taken as "coloured," or simply sunburnt? One explanation might be that she was a beautiful half-cast, whose angry brothers consigned her to a monotonous task, against which she rebelled in order to find greater freedom as a goatherd. If this is so, "vineyards" in the plural can be understood literally, but "mine own vineyard" is an erotic metaphor. She is an early example of a liberated woman who chooses her own lover.

But the coloured interpretation immediately comes up against a difficulty in chapter 2, when the female voice announces: –

I am a rose of Sharon, a lily of the valleys...

This is no doubt the lotus, not an appropriate metaphor for a black beauty. Perhaps their problem arises from family jealousies, which are hinted at: –

As a lily among thorns, so is my love among the daughters.

As the apple-tree among the trees of the wood, so is my beloved among the sons. (2, 2-5).

At this point, another consummation appears to occur: –

I sat down in his shadow with great delight, and his fruit was sweet to my taste. He brought me to the banqueting house, and his banner over me was love. (2, 3-4).

The lady is happily exhausted, and hungry: –

Stay me with raisins, comfort me with apples, for I am sick of love (=*malade d'amour* in the French versions, sick *with* love).

Over a distance of three or four thousand years, this plea may ring a bell with modern lovers, who remember picnicking in the small hours on what was left in the fruit-bowl or at the bottom of the fridge. But at the same time, love can be so intense that it becomes a pain, and should not be indulged in lightly: –

I adjure, O daughters of Jerusalem... that ye stir not up, nor awake love, till it please. (2, 7). (Don't be too forward, wait for the right moment or, more prosaically, don't wake him or her up, if asleep?).

The lovers now appear to be separated for a while, then he suddenly rushes back with all the panache of a young Lochinvar galloping out of the west. There follows, particularly in the English version, a perfect little prose poem about the urgency of desire: –

The voice of my beloved! Behold he cometh, leaping upon the mountains, skipping upon the hills.

My beloved spoke, and said unto me, rise up, my love, my fair one, and come away.

For lo, the winter is past, the rain is over and gone; the flowers appear on the earth: the time of the singing of birds has come, and the voice of the turtle is heard in our land.

Arise my love, my fair one, and come away.

However, since the course of true love never did run smooth, there is now an episode in the minor key, when the girl is sleeping alone and worried by unhappy dreams, and the lover is locked out: –

A garden shut up is my sister, my bride, a spring shut up, a fountain sealed. (4, 12).

After that, as in a mild nightmare, the images become increasingly blurred. The daughters of Jerusalem, turning querulous, question the uniqueness of the relationship between the lovers: –

What is thy beloved more than any other beloved that thou dost so adjure us? (6, 9).

Other wraith-like figures drift in and out of the text: a "Shulammite" of unknown origin, a prince's daughter, also anonymous, not to mention "threescore queens, fourscore concubines, and virgins without number." Despite this welter of femininity, the female voice continues to assert its faith: –

I am my beloved's, and my beloved is mine: he feedeth his flock among the lilies. (6, 3).

I am my beloved's, and his desire is towards me. (7, 10).

But the male voice – if it is the male voice – starts to mumble inarticulately: –

And thy mouth (is) like the best wine that goes down smoothly for my beloved, gliding through the lips of those that are asleep. (7, 9).

Faced with this somnambulist imbibing, the French commentaries take refuge in the usual verdict: "*texte incertain*."

So, what seemed to begin as a spring-time idyll, runs into the sands, rather in the way that the inspiration behind *Kubla Khan* dried up through the disastrous arrival of the person from Porlock. The Song of Songs cannot be praised, then, as a finished erotic masterpiece, but it certainly endures as a cluster of poetic fragments that the reader can use for the imaginative construction of his or her own poem of love.

8

Controversial Aspects of the Old Testament Myth

Looking back over the extraordinary jumble of the Old Testament, what can the sceptical modern reader pick out as the salient points he finds most difficult to accept?

To begin with, the symbolism of the Garden of Eden and the notion of original sin. Despite their powerful dramatic simplicity, they are at variance with the development of evolutionary thought since the Enlightenment. There never was a Garden of Eden or a Golden Age, in which fully developed man was securely established, before he made the mistake of offending God. Most people, even those who believe themselves to be religious, now conduct their lives on the assumption that "civilisation" has been an ever-repeated attempt to give a satisfactory pattern to human existence as it has moved, stage by stage, from its primitive to its more evolved forms. General satisfaction has never been achieved, and perhaps never will be, but the attempt has to go on.

In the past, various partial patterns of civilisation have come into being with their qualities and their defects, have lasted for a certain time, and then have yielded ground to others. By now, the whole world is joined up and, for the time being, for that very reason, is more incoherent than ever. But civilisation has always been unstable; it has made advances in some areas, and in others has suffered setbacks, and even at times local extinction. But there never was a Fall from a state of divine or natural grace, only the dogged struggle to survive and to move up, if possible, on the civilised scale.

The Jewish legend of the coming out of bondage to undertake the long and arduous journey to the Promised Land, although badly blurred by misconceptions and limiting peculiarities, can be seen – if we stand far enough back – as representative of the general human endeavour. At the risk of offending some Jews, we might say that, in a broad sense, we are all "Jews." The Promised Land still lies ahead; actually, it was never promised, or promised only by a fictitious, unreliable God; it is a human ideal, and belief in its future possibility is the essential act of faith.

The paradox of the Adam and Eve story is that they have to disobey God in order to start on the civilising process. The first effect of their eating of the apple from the Tree of Knowledge is that they become conscious of their nakedness. Unselfconscious exposure of the sexual organs is a characteristic of the animal kingdom. (And also, of course, of the non-conscious vegetable kingdom, where the sexual organs are a crowning glory; think of the Chelsea Flower Show.) Man being the only animal with articulate speech, is ambiguous about his animality; most of the time he tends to hide it or play it down, but on occasions he may let it rip, or flaunt it in a gesture of cosmic defiance. A flasher may be making a metaphysical statement.

Man, having language at his disposal, also has an urge to think, however inadequately. The God of the Old Testament is opposed to intellectual inquiry; he demands unthinking obedience. He anticipated what the Catholic Church was later to condemn as the *libido sciendi*, the illegitimate thirst for knowledge. But what are education, culture and civilisation if not a continuous diet of apples from the Tree of Knowledge? It is true that a little knowledge is a dangerous thing, but the danger can only be countered by more knowledge, provided we always bear in mind that, given the limitations of language as a human creation, knowledge framed in language is, at every stage, necessarily provisional. There is no escape from existential flux.

Another difficulty is that the God of the Old Testament is inadequate as a concept of the universal creator. He is a petty figure with a preference or a prejudice. Why should he need a Chosen People to dance attendance on him and attempt to do his bidding, when that bidding is often obscure, and sometimes openly immoral from any rational point of view? More importantly, why should the creator side with one part of his creation rather than with all parts? Presumably, because he himself is no more than a fiction engendered by the fear of life endemic, for some reason, among the prophets. Fear breeds superstition, and superstition breeds cruelty to others, and even towards oneself. How strange that, to appease the creator, humans should have felt the need to offer up animals, or other humans, or their children, and even themselves, as sacrificial victims in the illusory attempt to strike a bargain with the Unknown. According to anthropologists, there are, or there have been, savage tribes who, knowing that they have to kill and eat animals in order to survive, apologise to the "spirits" of these animals for being obliged to do so. This is surely more "civilised" than the gratuitous slaughter of lambs, rams and bullocks as burnt-offerings to provide "a sweet savour" for the nostrils of an imaginary Lord. No doubt the practice has long been abandoned, but it survives as a recurrent stain on the pages of the Old Testament.

In reading the prophets, I have often to overcome a feeling of repulsion, because even the minor ones, such as Nahum, Zephariah and Zechariah are full of anger and hatred. I have a particular dislike of the worst ranters, who are Ezra and Nehemiah. I can sympathise most with Jonah, the tragic-comic *prophète malgré lui*, who tries to elude the voice of God ordering him to go and preach doom to Nineveh. Instead, he escapes via Tarshish, but God pursues him relentlessly, raising a storm which causes Jonah to be thrown into the sea. God, still teleguiding the operation, causes Jonah to be swallowed by the whale. While in its belly, Jonah apologises to God on his mobile prophet-phone; he is duly vomited out onto dry land and told to carry on with his mission. He does so, announcing disaster within forty days. But the people of Nineveh undergo a miraculous change of heart and God, without warning Jonah, cancels the threat of the prophecy. Jonah suffers a nervous collapse and retires to a "booth" as a permanently deranged hermit. He has been crying "Wolf!" on God's behalf, and the unprecedented has happened; God has turned into a lamb. Like Job, Jonah has been let down by God, but in a different way.

Whatever we may say against the prophets, I suppose we have to admit that, in general, like the fanatical Christians of the Middle Ages, they at least kept alive the notion that there is a metaphysical dimension to life above the clash of the animal instincts related to secular power. The tragedy or the irony is that this awareness of the metaphysical dimension can produce perverted effects. When, in the episode I quoted earlier, Samuel demotes King Saul for disobedience and personally hacks Agag to pieces, he is establishing his spiritual authority over the secular authority of the monarch, but this spiritual authority is being used in such a benighted way that it becomes anti-spiritual.

. . . .

The commentaries of the catholic Bible of Jerusalem do their best to argue that the spirituality of the prophets is always predominantly pure, and they sum up the message of the Old Testament under three headings: *le monothéisme, le moralisme, l'attente du Salut* (monotheism, insistence on morality (?), waiting for salvation). All three points can be queried.

To say, as the Old Testament frequently does, that the Lord is the most powerful of the gods and that this constitutes his claim to worship, is to admit tacitly that there must be other gods with whom he is in competition. Occasionally, but grudgingly, the prophets hint at the idea that the Lord, being all powerful, must be Lord of the universe and consequently a creator valid for all nations, but they never proclaim this with total conviction as an overriding truth. They always come back to the special relationship with Israel. They agree that God moves in mysterious ways and is often incomprehensible, but they never arrive at the concept of "God" as a non-partisan, impersonal force running through all phenomena, animate and inanimate. He is always feared as a threatening presence, a mainly critical "watcher of men."

As for the morality of the Old Testament, there is no lack of evidence to demonstrate its confusions. The innocent may be involved in a blanket destruction; the guilty may remain unscathed. And it is particularly difficult to know what exactly is meant by "sin." More often than not, the word seems unconnected with the morality of personal relationships between human beings. Since it is coupled with the idea of "whoring after strange gods," it appears to be the failure to keep recognising the dominant Lord by a continuous chorus of praise backed up by burnt-offerings. In other words, it is primarily ritualistic. It does not allow for the possibility that an individual neglectful of ritual, or indifferent to it, may be a model of social virtue. It is further evidence of the overwhelming egotism of the fictional God thought up by the originators of the Old Testament.

As for the concept of salvation or redemption, it occurs most prominently in the volcanic explosion of the Book of Isaiah, one of the longest in the Bible, a sort of prophetic lava-flow of rhetoric, which seems to contain, cheek by jowl, everything and its opposite. Given the disparities in time of the historical references, the French commentators agree that it cannot be the work of a single person; they posit three possible Isaiahs, not to mention other putative minor contributors.

The central thread is, as usual, the repeated assertion of the all-powerfulness of the God of Israel, and his chequered relationship with the Chosen People, whom he sometimes supports in their contentious relations with the surrounding nations, and sometimes, if he is displeased, allows to be taken into bondage, or punished in other ways. But here, in part of the book at least (chapter 40 *et seq*) God is in a relatively genial and forgiving mood – he is singing "a new song" – and he makes some encouraging promises in relation to the future. According to the Jerusalem Bible, chapter 40, and those immediately following, can be referred to as the Book of Consolation, because God, the harsh taskmaster, is suddenly converted to God, the carer: –

Comfort ye, comfort ye my people, saith your God. Speak ye comfortably to Jerusalem, and cry unto her that her warfare is accomplished, that her iniquity is pardoned; that she hath received of the Lord's hands double for all her sins. (40, 1, 2).

(Presumably, this last phrase means: a double award, in spite of her sins?)

The switch from sternness to amenity is quite sudden because, in the immediately preceding chapter 39, King Hezekiah, who has vexed the Lord by fraternising ever so slightly with the son of the King of Babylon, is told by Isaiah what punishment will ensue: –

Behold, the days come, that all that is in thy house and which thy fathers have laid in store until this day, shall be carried to Babylon: nothing shall be left, saith the Lord.

And of thy sons that shall issue from thee, which thou shalt beget, shall they take away; and they shall be eunuchs in the palace of the King of Babylon.

To which Hezekiah makes the extraordinary reply: –

Good is the word of the Lord which thou hast spoken... For there shall be peace and truth in my days (39, 6-8).

He seems to have been rendered incoherent by the shock.

But even in chapter 40, God, in his supposedly benevolent mood, emphasizes that humanity is like grass which withereth, and boasts about his own immortal strength: –

Behold, the Lord God will come as a mighty one, and his arm shall rule for him.

Before devoting two further chapters to the blowing of his own trumpet, God – for the duration of a single verse – resorts to the hypocritical pastoral metaphor: –

He shall feed his flock like a shepherd, he shall gather the lambs in his arms and carry them in his bosom, and shall gently lead those (the ewes?) that give suck. (40, 11).

The flock is still the Chosen People, not humanity as a whole: –

Fear not, thou worm Jacob, and ye men of Israel; I will help thee, saith the Lord, and thy redeemer is the Holy One of Israel. (41, 14).

This is the first occurrence in Isaiah of the word, "redeemer," which is later repeated several times. It leads us into another major biblical puzzle: who is the "redeemer" and what exactly is his function? The commentators in the French bibles explain that the Hebrew word is *"go-el,"* and they translate it by *"le racheteur"*[19]. It is a legal term,

---

[19] The Bayard Version: –
ne crains rien, larve de Jacob
avorton d'Israël
Je viens à ton secours (cont. over)

covering a number of defensive functions: avenging the death of a kinsman, "raising up seed" to his memory, (Boaz is the "defender" of Ruth), paying his debts, buying him out of slavery, and so on. If the Lord is the Holy One of Israel and also the redeemer, this must mean that he has spontaneously decided to wipe the slate clean, to forgive Israel's "transgressions" in an *acte gratuit* which demands no counterpart. He keeps this up for a while; in chapter 41, he promises to make the desert bloom like a rose, while he is utterly destroying the enemies of Israel.

In chapter 42, there is a change of tone. A mysterious intermediary character is suddenly introduced: –

> Behold my servant, whom I uphold; my chosen, in whom my soul delighteth: I have put my spirit upon him; he shall bring forth judgement to the Gentiles.
>
> He shall not fail nor be discouraged, till he have set judgement in the earth, and the isles shall wait for his law.

God promises support for this redeemer, who is now, apparently, other than himself.

> I the Lord have called thee in righteousness, and will hold thine hand, and will keep thee, and give thee for a covenant of the people, for a light of the Gentiles. (42, 1,4,6).

This has generally been taken as the first prophetic hint of the future Messiah. As the tide of words flows on, he gets lost at times in the froth and the foam, but he surfaces again in chapters 53 and 61, where he is referred to in the third person: –

- déclaration de Yhwh –
ton racheteur, c'est le Saint d'Israël.
The Jerusalem Bible: –
Ne crains rien, vermisseau de Jacob
et vous, pauvres gens d'Israël,
c'est moi qui te viens en aide, oracle de Yahvé,
Celui qui te rachète, c'est le Saint d'Israël.

... he was wounded for our transgressions, he was bruised for our iniquities: the chastisement of our peace was upon him (?); and with his stripes we are healed. (53, 4, 5).

In chapter 61, he speaks openly in his own voice as the redeemer: –
The spirit of the Lord God is upon me: because the Lord hath appointed me to preach good tidings unto the meek: he hath sent me to bind up the broken-hearted, to proclaim liberty to the captives, and the opening of the prison to them that are bound. (61, 1).

In the first of these last two quotations, redemption takes on a rather different meaning. The pardon granted by the Lord may be spontaneous, but it is no longer unconditional. It involves a *quid pro quo*, a sacrifice; the Messiah, if it is he, is at once a messenger of reconciliation and a scapegoat, the God/Man equivalent of a burnt-offering. This will eventually be stated quite clearly in the New Testament, (John, 1, 20): "Behold the Lamb of God, which taketh away the sin of the world." For the moment, in Isaiah, the fact is disguised by another hypocritical use of the pastoral metaphor, this time in its vegetable mode: –
For as the earth bringeth forth her bud, and as the garden causeth the things that are sown in it to bring forth; so the Lord God will cause righteousness and praise (for himself?) to spring forth before all the nations. (61, 11).

Within the context of the Book of Isaiah, the promise of peace and universalisation remains unfulfilled. The message continues to be contradictory to the very end. Isaiah, whether he was one man or a cluster of discordant prophets, cannot rid himself of the incubus of the God of Fear. What could be more dispiriting than the final chapter?: –
For behold, the Lord will come with fire, and his chariots shall be like the whirlwind; to render his anger with fury, and his rebuke with flashes of fire.

And it shall come to pass that from one new moon to another, and from one Sabbath to another, shall all flesh come to worship before me, saith the Lord.

And they shall go forth, and look upon the carcasses of the men that have transgressed against me; for their worm shall not die, neither shall their fire be quenched; and they shall be an abhorring unto all flesh. (66, 14,16, 23, 24).

It is astonishing that Jesus – whatever his own ambiguities that I shall refer to later – while never openly coming out against the Old Testament, somehow managed to transcend the sadistic muddle of Isaiah, and to create an evangelistic message of universal love. From the strictly intellectual point of view, it may be no more tenable than the opposite concept of the susceptible, avenging God, but at least it never advocates killing as a habitual procedure, and it tends to minimise suffering rather than increase it.

. . . .

While we are on the subject of Isaiah, I would like to comment further on the puzzle connected with the use of the word "redeemer." In the English Bible it forms a sort of bridge between the Old Testament and the New but, curiously enough, it does not have this function either in the Bayard Version or in the Jerusalem Bible. In the English-speaking world, it is also familiar through its use in Handel's oratorio, the *Messiah*, one of the most popular musical works based on the Bible, and which, fortunately – such is the independent power of music – can be enjoyed by non-believers as well as believers. The libretto is a compilation of texts taken from different parts of the Scriptures, and one of the highlights of the work is the thrilling soprano solo: "I know that my Redeemer liveth." It was traditionally thought that the compiler of the libretto was a certain Charles Jennens, a wealthy landowner who sent it to Handel, but it is now believed to have been put together by a Doctor Pooley, chaplain and secretary to Jennens; the latter deserves no credit for it.

The other great highlight of the work, the Hallellujah Chorus, comes from the Book of Revelation, the last book of the New Testament, where the continued but fainter presence of the Lord God is softened by association with Jesus Christ. But where did Pooley find "I know that my Redeemer liveth"? The sentence is usually understood as referring to Jesus, particularly since it is followed by a quotation from Corinthians I, 15, 20: – "For now is Christ risen from the dead..." But if you consult *Cruden's Concordance*, you discover that "redeemer" as a personal noun does not occur in the New Testament, but only in the Old. The New Testament has the verb "to redeem" and the verbal noun "redemption," but no redeemer. On asking around, I have not found one person who could place the quotation correctly. The usual answer is: "From the New Testament or the Psalms".

Actually, the phrase "I know that my redeemer liveth" comes from the most unlikely of all sources, the book of Job (Ch.19, 25 *et seq*), where it occurs unexpectedly *comme un cheveu sur la soupe, et quel cheveu!* The whole passage is as mysterious as anything else in the Bible: –

Have pity on me, O ye my friends; for the hand of God hath touched me.

Why do you persecute me as God, and are not satisfied with my flesh?

Oh, that my words were now written!

Oh, that they be inscribed in a book!

That with an iron pen and lead they were graven in the rock forever!

But I know that my Redeemer liveth, and that he shall stand up at last upon the earth:

And after my skin has been destroyed, yet from my flesh shall I see God: whom I shall see for myself, and mine eyes shall behold and not another. My reins are consumed within me.

(Authorised Version: – He shall stand at the latter day upon the earth, and although worms destroy this body, yet in my flesh shall I see God.)

Job is, for the moment, in open disagreement with the God of Israel. Why, then, this sudden beam of hope lighting up the dark night of the soul? It is as if Job were positing the existence of a different, more just God than the familiar God of Israel. Simone Weil, religious but not orthodox, has a touching expression which may be applicable here. She says somewhere that the human soul always expects good to be done to it rather than evil, and is wounded when this is not the case. She may mean that, in the worst distress, the soul is bound to imagine a second redeemer – in cricketing terms, the long-stop – if the first redeemer has failed. Job will see the true God and not "another"; "another" = the God of Israel?

The French commentators are embarrassed by the passage, for which they can offer no convincing explanation. But they can avoid the sudden eruption of the Christian Redeemer in the Book of Job – *le Christ rédempteur* – by keeping to the weaker terms: –

Bayard Version: – *Je sais que mon Défenseur est vivant.*

Jerusalem Bible: – *Je le sais, mon racheteur vit.*

It would have been interesting to know if Pooley, with deliberate intent, plucked the verse from the most anti-God book of the Old Testament to enable it to become an eloquent profession of faith associated with the New. Had he not wrenched Job out of context, the *Messiah* might well have been a rather different work. Therefore, he has his modest but effective place in the creation of the masterpiece, alongside the two geniuses, Handel the originator of the music, and Mozart the reviser.

9

Comparing the Two Myths

When I was a child, I felt that to pass from the Old Testament to the New was like coming out of a dark tunnel into relatively bright daylight. They were both fairy-tales, of course, because they abounded in improbable events called miracles and moved inconsequentially from point to point. But the first was a sombre tale with few cheerful moments. Its dominant character was a tetchy old man in the sky with an inordinate thirst for praise and always ready to pounce on poor humanity, reason or no reason. In the New Testament, the Son had taken over, and this was a great relief. The heavens ceased to be threatening, the frequency of human and animal slaughter came to an end, and the stench of burnt offerings evaporated. Instead of thundering from on high, the Son wandered busily around the everyday world, healing the sick, raising the dead, and telling everybody what a nice person his Father really was. I enjoyed the change of atmosphere, but I remained unconvinced. How well did the Son actually know the Father?

By the age of seven, I guessed that Jesus must be a fiction, like any other fairy-tale figure. I was incapable of believing in his miracles, because I knew that no amount of faith on my part would prevent the fierce westerly gale blasting along the Roman Wall from knocking me off my feet, if I did not keep to the lee of the dry-stone dykes separating the fields. And why raise people from the dead, if they were only going to die again afterwards? This was no explanation of the mystery of life and death. As for the lilies of the field which toil not, neither do they spin, if the adults around me had not toiled, there would have been nothing to eat; our loaves and fishes were not indefinitely extensible.

Jesus was a likeable character. He was sound about the idiocy of the strict application of the sabbath rule, his heart was in the right place – "let him who is without sin cast the first stone" – but all his exploits and some of his sayings had to be taken with a pinch of salt.

However, my present reading of the Gospels has caused me some surprise. Although I have never had any faith, I did not realise how much of the text I knew by heart, and how many biblical expressions are part and parcel of my everyday secular thinking. Like the old lady who saw a performance of *Hamlet* for the first time and complained: "But it's all quotations!", I am tempted to exclaim at the *déjà-vu*. I have to admit that the Gospels marked me for life, and this must prove something about the power of their language, independently of religious belief.

Yet my basic rational objection has not been weakened, but rather confirmed. For instance, chapter one of Matthew begins with a glaring misstatement I had not noticed before. We are told that Jesus Christ was "the son of David". There follows a long genealogy establishing a filiation, through the two most famous kings of Israel, David and Solomon, with Joseph, the husband of Mary. But Joseph's origins are completely irrelevant, since the great central point of the Gospels is that he is *not* the father of Jesus. He had refrained from "knowing" Mary. God, behaving like an adulterous Jupiter, had artificially inseminated her, presumably by means of the Holy Ghost, so that Joseph, with his supposedly royal blood, is completely out of the picture. Since Mary is not credited with any distinguished ancestors, Jesus is a commoner on his mother's side. But the Three Wise Men turn up immediately to proclaim him king on the mystic level, so that we can enjoy the pathos of a royal baby cradled in a manger. I know of a couple who had to cradle their first-born in an empty drawer for want of a proper receptacle, but since no royal aura was present, the pathos was negligible. Later in the Matthew Gospel, and again in Mark, Jesus continues to be referred to as "the son of David". Although he is incarnated as a humble mortal, his publicity benefits from two royal lines, one human, the other divine.

Then, that all-important event, the Holy Impregnation, comes in two odd versions, one in Matthew, the other in Luke. In Matthew, Joseph is perturbed, as well he might be, on discovering that his betrothed is pregnant. We are not told how he found this out, or what Mary had to say by way of explanation. After a man-to-man talk with the Angel, Joseph allows himself to be reassured. He does not make the fuss that might have been expected from Job or Jonah in a comparable situation. Perhaps he took the line that to be cuckolded by God Almighty, without so much as a by-your-leave, was an honour, just as, at the court of Louis XIV, some husbands may have been pleased when the Sun King singled out their wives for attention.

In the second version, it is Mary who receives the visit from the Angel to tell her of God's will. If I remember rightly, in at least one old painting, the creative act is depicted as a delicate streak of silver from Heaven. Again surprisingly, there is no discussion between the spouses (presumably, by this point they are married), but Mary goes to visit Elizabeth who, long past the menopause, is heavily pregnant with John the Baptist. John, sensing the proximity of the embryonic Christ, leaps in the womb, and both women take this as a "sign". Actually, this hardly counts as a "sign," because even ordinary babies tend to be vigorous in the later stages of pregnancy, as some fathers can testify, having been kicked awake in the night by their impatient progeny in a hurry to be born. The "sign," if there is one, is the elderly woman's pregnancy, a routine miracle copied from the Old Testament, because of the belief that a childless woman has not fulfilled her purpose in life.

But there is no point in expecting verisimilitude in the details when all is myth. The details are just coherent or incoherent aspects of the underlying symbolism. Although the New Testament is shorter than the Old (one quarter of the whole Bible), its symbolism is rather more complex, since it operates on two levels. The Old Testament deals essentially with the contentious relationship between the Lord and his Chosen People, either collectively or as represented by certain individuals. The New Testament relegates God more or less to the wings, from which he communicates from time to time with Jesus; there is a God-Jesus conjunction. But Jesus is predominantly in the world and makes remarks about it as a man. It is convenient to consider these two aspects – the metaphysical and the social – separately, although they are constantly interlinked.

. . . .

I argued earlier that the decision of the Bayard editors to rename the two Testaments *Alliance* and *Nouvelle Alliance* was unjustified, because there can be no such thing as a covenant between humanity on the one hand, and the unreachable Transcendent on the other. Let me emphasise this all-important point once again. Older readers will remember that just before the Second World War, the English Prime Minister, Neville Chamberlain, came back from his vital meeting with Adolf Hitler gleefully waving a piece of paper and saying that he had reached an agreement with the German dictator. Almost immediately the agreement proved to be an illusion, but at least Chamberlain was correct in saying that he had a document signed by Hitler. In the case of the supposed covenant with God, there is no documentary evidence. The Tables of Stone can have been no more than a metaphor, or at best a forgery. Moses, or whoever it was, composed the text, and guaranteed it, arbitrarily and one-sidedly, on God's behalf. Jesus, making a similar, but even greater, use of supposed miracles, does the same.

The real link between the two Testaments is not so much the imaginary covenant as the concept of Redemption, which is real in the sense that it has had an effect as an operative idea, but is also just as imaginary, since it is part of the gratuitous mythic structure. Why should man need redemption? Because of the doctrine of original sin, which is a myth purporting to explain the existence of moral evil in the world by putting the blame firmly on humanity.

God, we may say, is sadistic from the start; he inaugurates human life with a prohibition, knowing full well – since he can see into the future – that it will be violated, because of the curiosity he has also instilled in human nature. In spite of his assertions to the contrary, he is not a merciful God, because he expels Adam and Eve at once, without offering them a second chance. Even worse, he makes the fault hereditary. Every human is born with the stain of the original sin, and is expected to struggle against it: "created sick, commanded to be sound". The recommended course of action is to praise God incessantly, to obey his will if you are lucky enough to know what it is, and to offer up sacrifices.

As we have seen, in the hurly-burly of Isaiah, God suddenly and unexpectedly softens his attitude. He declares himself to be spontaneously reconciled with his Chosen People; he himself will be their Redeemer. However, he doesn't explain what this means; is he going to relieve Israel of the burden of original sin? A little later, he forgets that he has promised to be the Redeemer, and instead floats the idea of a future special representative, who will have his entire approval. This eventually turns out to be Christ, the Messiah, because God, making one of his rare but dramatic appearances in the New Testament, describes Jesus as "my only begotten son in whom I am well pleased". Incidentally, "only begotten" is another piece of false pathos like "cradled in a manger". God, the creator, can obviously beget as many children as he likes, and besides he already has a troop of sons in Heaven, as we learned at the beginning of the Book of Job[20].

At first, the essential aspect of the role of Jesus, the Messiah, is not stressed. His primary function is to perform miracles as "signs" of his divine origin under the direct patronage of God, so as to impress the backsliders among the Chosen People and return them to the true faith. His mission is not yet universal or tragic. But it gradually emerges from the threats that begin to surround him, from what he himself says and from the intimations picked up by his disciples, that his ultimate destiny is to be a sacrificial victim. We have here a more elaborate reenactment of the Abraham scenario in the Old Testament. Young Isaac is reprieved at the last moment, and the ram takes his place. But, in dealing with his own "Son," "God" allows the sacrifice to go ahead with all its appalling details. It is as if the Abraham episode had been a first dummy run, an obscure happening in a remote field witnessed by no-one. With the Crucifixion, the stage-management is vastly improved. The sacrifice is a public execution, watched by a crowd of onlookers, including the victim's mother: *stabat mater*. There is the pleasing equilibrium of the three crosses, – 3 is perhaps the most fundamental of the "magic" numbers – the central cross for the divine innocent with his crown of thorns, and the two side ones for the common criminals. A crucifixion is not over in a moment with disappointing rapidity, like a beheading; it has its successive phases, the dragging of the cumbersome instrument of torture to the place of execution, the waiting for the slow death, and

---

[20] God is forgetful. He refers to Isaac as Abraham's "only son". Yet he himself sent an angel to Hagar, the handmaid, to announce that she would give birth to Ishmael, Abraham's elder son.

then the pathetic poses of the body as it is lowered to the ground. All this wallowing in cruelty and suffering, as related in the text and as portrayed imaginatively in centuries of religious painting, in the end makes the New Testament just as repugnant to the secular mind as the Old Testament. I have never understood why the sado-masochistic symbol of the crucifix should continue to be displayed so widely, as if it were conducive to healthy, loving thoughts; still less, why the bleeding Sacred Heart should be the cherished image of certain Catholic communities.

Apart from the repulsive iconography, is it not an unacceptable, barbaric notion that one individual can, or should be made a scape-goat for the benefit of all? Besides, in the Old Testament, the concept of redemption remains inextricably muddled, and it is not made much clearer in the New. God, who at first makes the promise that he himself will be the Redeemer, fails to explain what he means by this. Surely, if we think for a moment within the terms of the myth, the only thing that man needs to be redeemed from is original sin, which God inflicted on him in the first place. Original sin itself is a puzzle; if it means a natural tendency to wickedness, it is unevenly distributed; some people, by their very nature, are more wicked, that is, more anti-social, than others. God, if he existed, could redeem man by abolishing the tendency to deliberate wickedness. There would remain simply the human tendency to err, which would be enough to account for human evil, without the extra burden of original sin as an incurable negative urge.

The pitch is queered by the fact that God forgets his promise, or cannot think of a way of carrying it out, and so he passes on the onus to Jesus. Jesus is duly crucified with pomp and circumstance, but to placate whom and for what? It must be to placate God himself because, within the vicious circle of the myth, all sacrifices are addressed to him. However, the martyrdom of Jesus does not produce redemption on earth. God does not reciprocate by cancelling out original sin or doing anything else in return. Man still remains sinful by definition, and redemption is postponed until the next world. It will be enjoyed by those who, in this world, have faith in the Father and the Son; they can expect to suffer accordingly at the hands of the wicked, even to the point of martyrdom, which they should accept gladly in the name of Jesus. Redemption has been described crudely, but with some justification, as "pie in the sky". But we have no information about the ingredients in the pie of heavenly bliss.

What Jesus contributes to the myth is a *promise*, the promise of the after-life: –

In my father's house are many mansions.

... I go to prepare a place for you. (John, 14. 2.)

I have already mentioned that there is no such promise in the Old Testament. Heaven is the abode of God and his angels, and is not generally accessible to humans, however virtuous. Elijah is the only character who drives off in that direction, but his precise destination is not specified. When men set about building a tower in order to reach Heaven, God punishes their presumption by turning it into the Tower of Babel. According to the Old Testament, after death, humans may go down into Sheol or "the pit", a sort of ill-defined purgatory or limbo, the function of which remains obscure, or they "sleep with their fathers" in the soil of the earth. The comforting phrase "to sleep in Abraham's bosom" occurs only in the New Testament (Luke, 16. 22.), with a corresponding reference to Hell fire. It is a curious feature of the Old Testament God that he is not metaphysically inclined. He rewards some individuals or tribes, and occasionally the Chosen People as a whole, but only by granting them prosperity in the here-and-now, and promising them a numerous progeny in the future. When he punishes, he does not make use of the threat of Hell, but promptly sends down fire and pestilence. The New Testament refers more clearly than the Old to the opposition between Heaven and Hell (see Matthew, *passim*). The righteous shall enter into eternal life, but the wrong-doers shall suffer eternal punishment and be burned like chaff in the eternal fire. Christ, without being a thorough-going Hell-fire preacher like some of the baleful divines of the later Christian tradition, is not always "Gentle Jesus, meek and mild".

. . . .

But did he exist? As we saw from the commentary in the Bayard Version, which may be heretical, of course, from the orthodox Catholic point of view, even some believers now doubt the existence of a single, historical Jesus. He may be a composite figure that the collective imagination has fused together out of several *illuminés* or religious eccentrics. Perhaps so, but on my present re-reading, particularly of the Gospel according to St. John, which I find the most harrowing of the four, I sense a strange human pathos. The text portrays a strongly marked character, in the grip of what might be called God-obsessed dementia. It has a neurotic intensity, which seems to be emanating from a single individual.

He presents himself as a temporary, alien visitor to this planet: –
Ye are of this world. I am not of this world. (18. 23.)
The distinction between Father and Son is obliterated: –
I and the Father are one. (10. 30)
Jesus, like God, has existed from all eternity: –
Before Abraham was, I am. (8. 58.)
Since the orthodox are against him – "a prophet hath no honour in his own country" – he has a broader vision than the Old Testament God. He sees beyond the Chosen People, and believes himself to be the saviour of the whole world: –
And other sheep I have, which are not of this fold; them also must I bring, and they shall hear my voice, and they shall become one flock, one shepherd. (10. 16.)

The suspicion that, by now, he is not altogether sane is increased by a further, and quite absurd, use of the pastoral metaphor, which all along has been exploited with various degrees of accuracy or inaccuracy in both Testaments. Jesus oscillates schizophrenically between two notions; he is at once the good shepherd and the sacrificial lamb: –

I am the good shepherd. The good shepherd layeth down his life for the sheep.
He that is a hireling, and not a shepherd, whose own the sheep are not, beholdeth the wolf coming and leaveth the sheep and fleeth, and the wolf snatcheth them, and scattereth them. (10. 11. 12.)

Surely this is sentimental nonsense. I doubt whether any shepherd has ever laid down his life, except perhaps in resisting cattle-rustlers. A conscientious hireling would put up a fight against one wolf, but if he were outnumbered by a pack of wolves, the sensible course would be to run for help, rather than let himself be killed to no purpose. Besides, as I have already had occasion to point out, the pastoral metaphor is fundamentally hypocritical. The sheep are not being protected for their own sake, but because they are a human possession. For all we know, they may prefer to be eaten by wolves rather than by humans.

Jesus, the-man-who-would-be-God, seems suddenly more egotistical in his megalomania: –

I am the way, the truth and the life: no-one comes unto the Father, but by me. (14. 6.)

Why this bottle-neck? Holy babe in the manger becomes holy dog in the manger?

He is torn between two possibilities. He wants to enjoy the glory of being the sacrificial lamb. The word "glorified" occurs several times: –

The hour is come that the Son of Man should be glorified. (12. 23.)

But he has moments of human revulsion: –

Now my soul is troubled; and what shall I say? Father, save me from this hour? But for this cause came I to this hour. (12. 27.)

There are hints that he is psyching himself up to reassurance. He expects to return to earth "in a little while"; people now living will see him come back in all his glory, attended by angels. In the end, he positively connives at his own death. He says to Judas: "What thou doest, do quickly," as if he were impatient to get through the ordeal and to take his place in Heaven as soon as possible. He stubbornly refuses to respond to Pilate's civilised overtures, although Pilate is trying to save him.[21] If I may be allowed a little blasphemy, I would suggest that, in effect, Jesus committed suicide through the combination of two motives: the attempt to live out the idea of Redemption, although, as we have seen, it is adumbrated in hopelessly obscure and unsatisfactory terms both in Isaiah and in the New Testament, and the mad desire as a human to reach divine status. Historically, the combination of the two motives has proved an enormous mythic success the world over, perhaps because the underlying emotions, however contorted the forms they may take, are love and hope, whereas the leitmotiv of the Old Testament is fear, which tends to make fewer converts.

. . . .

---

[21] Pilate is one of the most intriguing characters in the Bible. He makes his mark with only very few words in each Gospel, and the symbolic washing of the hands in Matthew. I am not sure that Francis Bacon's famous reference to him – "What is truth? said jesting Pilate, and would not stay for an answer" – does him justice. When he put the question (John, 18. 38.), it may have been with serious ironic intent. From the point of view of an enlightened administrator who probably had no more belief in the Roman gods than in the Jewish God, the inter-Jewish quarrel he had to cope with must have seemed to be a tedious clash between two equally gratuitous superstitions.

In the Gospel according to St. John, Jesus remains generally *au-dessus de la mêlée*, as regards social matters. His final recommendations to the disciples stress the concept of love and encourage the practice of healing that he claims to have instilled in them, but their action is to be predominantly evangelical on the metaphysical level. There is still no emphasis on social change in the world.[22] Jesus repeats the statement already made in Matthew and Mark: "The poor ye have always with you."

However, in the main body of the Gospels, Jesus is so clearly on the side of the underdog, in a way the Old Testament is not, that it is possible to disregard his wonder-working as a picturesque adornment, in order to concentrate on what might seem to be his rebellious social message. I guess that this may have been the case with my father, who gave up his Methodist local preaching to become a militant socialist. Or perhaps he became impatient with the other-worldliness of the Christian message and half lost his religious faith. He and his friends and his associates, with him as the ring-leader[23],

---

[22] In *Leviathan*, Hobbes quotes Christ's quietism with approval, and gets himself into a philosophical knot: – "... our Saviour gave them (the Apostles) the power to preach and baptise in all parts of the world, supposing they were not by their lawful Sovereign forbidden; for to our lawful Sovereign, Christ himself and his Apostles have in sundry places expressly commanded in all things to be obedient."

This, as I have said, supposes that "lawful" has an absolute meaning, guaranteed presumably by "God" or by "Nature," two doubtful concepts in which Hobbes is putting his trust. When, through the fortunes of war, Cromwell replaced Charles I as the "lawful" sovereign, was it incumbent on every Englishman automatically to change his allegiance? Pragmatic acceptance of the new status quo may coexist alongside moral reservations.

[23] They could be called "working-class intellectuals". There were many others like them in those serious days. They formed the backbone of the Labour Movement, with the help of some good-hearted upper-middle-class intellectuals who appeared from time to time like beings from another world, speaking a different kind of English. Since they often stayed overnight, I remember the names of some of the female militants who had a kind word for the little boy who gaped at them: Susan Lawrence, Margaret Bondfield, Mrs. Bruce-Glazier.

still sang some hymns around the American organ, but their favourite song undoubtedly was *The Red Flag*. They belonged to a radical group called the Independent Labour Party. I never overheard them discussing religion; their talk was all about Keir Hardie, Philip Snowden, Jimmy Maxwell and, of course, Ramsay MacDonald and the Great Betrayal. To them, the Old Testament must have seemed quite upper-class. It is full of kings, judges and prophets; the Lord in Heaven is top king, but there are many others beneath him on earth, and it is remarkable how many of the Old Testament figures serve both the Lord above and the terrestrial monarchs below, some of them non-Jewish: – Joseph and Moses - the Pharaohs; Samuel – King Saul; Nathan – David and Solomon; Mordecai – Ahasuerus, etc. Jesus is given the honorary or derisory title of "King of the Jews," but he never consorts with important people; he recruits his own party of the God-obsessed from among the humble. Nor, unlike some of his Old Testament predecessors, does he live in bondage, comfortable or otherwise, abroad. He is in his own country, but it is occupied territory, where he is subject to three authorities: the subservient Jewish royal administration, the orthodox Jewish church and the over-riding imperial rule of Rome.

According to the biblical story, his only determined enemies were the orthodox Jews, who opposed him on two counts: he blasphemed by claiming to be not simply a messenger, a Messiah, but the Son of God; by stirring up popular excitement, he might endanger the provisional balance with Rome. The civil authority, however, was neutral: the Herod of his adult years did not seek to kill him like the Herod of his infancy, but asked to see him out of curiosity and found him harmless, as did Pilate.

Jesus certainly never preached sedition. The promises of the Sermon on the Mount all relate to blessedness at some unknown future date, most probably in the next world. The meek will inherit the earth, but only in God's good time. The rich are encouraged to rid themselves of their wealth to enhance their spirituality, but even they may go with their camels through the eye of the needle, if such is God's will, since he can do all things. Jesus is absolutely opposed to violence, even in self-defence, as when he says one should turn the other cheek, or he orders Simon Peter to put up his sword during the scene of the arrest (one wonders why a disciple of Christ happened to be equipped with a sword; another biblical mystery?).

In short, Jesus is a total Quietist, with no sense of what would now be called political activism or resistance to oppression. Furthermore, despite his initial connection with carpentry, he was never part of the average working population. He has a "hippy," mendicant aspect, which is contrary to ordinary working-class morality. He prefers Mary to Martha[24], whereas it is the Marthas of this world, whether female or male, who do the chores, and sustain life from day to day. The phrase *laborare est orare* was invented long after Christ's death, and it is not certain that he would have approved of it. The monks, whose motto it was, could be suspected of resorting unconsciously to physical exhaustion as a way of dealing with their *acedia* or attacks of metaphysical doubt.

. . . .

At first sight, it is one of the great paradoxes of history that Jesus, the

---

[24] There is a complication in this contrast between the Marthas and the Marys. "Man does not live by bread alone" is perhaps Christ's most luminous aphorism. Some of the Marys of this world are unproductive drones – *des fruits secs* is an appropriate French expression – of no benefit to society. Others may be vital to civilisation. By accepting the charity of benefactors with apparent laziness, or in living by expedients and with a degree of amorality, they may be protecting an artistic or intellectual talent which might be killed by routine, but which may eventually flower to the advantage of culture as a whole. The Marys should not be judged too hastily. It is impossible to tell a priori to which of the two categories – positive or negative – a given individual belongs.

Quietist and the "hippy," should have inspired so much conflict and activism. I would tentatively suggest one or two possible causes of this phenomenon.

In the first place, if you assure the meek that they will eventually inherit the earth, they may become less meek, through the realisation that they are in the majority, and that their collective strength may allow them to come into their inheritance sooner rather than later. A bird in the hand is worth two in the bush. Christian Socialists aimed – and perhaps still do – at happiness for all in the here and now, and left it to God to ensure bliss in the hereafter. Also, among the underdogs, there are always some potential top dogs who are not at all meek, and who may seize the opportunity offered by social unrest to organise a new hierarchy or hierarchies, according to the number of top dogs contending with each other. In modern European history, Napoleon remains the outstanding illustration of this possibility, with Lenin, Stalin and Hitler trailing at some distance behind him.

Napoleon, as it happened, was without a shred of religious belief, but he manipulated religion skilfully for political purposes, moving the Pope about like a figure on a chess-board. He trusted superstitiously in his lucky star which, in the end, let him down. Lenin and Stalin obviously had no religion, "the opium of the people"; being devoid of human warmth, they presumably believed only in themselves and dressed up this belief in a convenient political ideology, to be applied dogmatically. As for Hitler, hidden away in his mad subconscious, these may have been a neo-Semitic conviction that the "Aryan" tribe was the real "Chosen People".

The situation is most confused when two doggedly pious leaders confront each other, both equally convinced that "God" is on his side. Then, religion becomes so inextricably interwoven with economic problems and reasons of state that historians can go on indefinitely reassessing the relative importance of the different elements in producing the crisis, whether it be civil war or international strife.

Disregarding for the moment the interlocking complexities of English history in the seventeenth century, we can perhaps see the opposition between Charles I and Cromwell as an exemplary instance: Charles, the Catholic, secure in his belief in the Divine Right of Kings, and Cromwell, with as violently neurotic a temperament as an Old Testament prophet, second-guessing God's Providence at every turn. In the end, the victory went to Cromwell, who with some qualms, agreed to Charles's execution, and Charles died with dignity as a Christian gentleman. Had Charles won, he, without qualms, would no doubt have found it necessary to execute Cromwell, and Cromwell might have gone to his death with equal fortitude.[25] But, had religious dogmatism not been operative on both sides, constitutional monarchy might have been arrived at earlier without the roundabout process of civil war, regicide and restoration.[26]

However, this suggestion may be too optimistic. I have been emphasising the harmfulness of dogmatic religion in propagating false myths. But it has to be admitted that religion is only one form of myth and, in a given situation, it may not be the most harmful. There is also the myth of power and possession, which may strike even deeper than the religious myth and, from the Absurdist point of view, it may be more difficult to dispel. Let me explain what I mean by a brief comment on Christ's famous maxim: "Render unto Caesar the things that are Caesar's and unto God the things that are God's". (Mat. 22. 17.)

---

[25] Cromwell was in fact executed, but posthumously. After the Restoration his body was dug up and hanged at Tyburn.

[26] The French Revolution of 1789 is different. Reduced to its simplest expression, it can be seen as a clash between the Divine Right of Kings, represented by the absolute monarchy, and the principle of reason. Unfortunately, reason, after being sane during the Enlightenment, went mad for a time and became the avenging Goddess of Reason, celebrated by feasts.

The Pharisees, to embarrass him and in the hope of jeopardising his relationship with the authorities, had asked him if it was lawful to pay tribute to Caesar. His answer is wily, but does it go to the root of the matter? "The things that Caesar's," that is, the right to exact tribute, had been won by armed conquest; Caesar was not entitled to the tribute in any absolute sense. He was just temporarily in authority over territory that had been wrested from others by force. If we make a comparison with twentieth-century Europe, we can say that, for a while, Hitler was Caesar in France, and his reign was iniquitous, not relatively innocuous like Caesar's in the Palestine of those days; as we have seen, Pilate was an enlightened colonial administrator. Therefore Jesus had right on his side in implying that it was better to keep the peace by paying the tribute. But had he been in France during the Nazi occupation, his quietist answer might not have seemed so convincing.

To emphasise the point, I can quote a real-life incident. A French colleague, a former member of the Resistance Movement, told me that he had been part of a delegation which went to ask the very Catholic writer, Paul Claudel, an outstanding figure at the time, if he could help in any way. Since he was elderly and living in retirement, they did not expect him to do anything concrete, but they thought that the authority of his fame and his status as an ex-ambassador to Washington might allow him to make a symbolic declaration or gesture without danger to himself. But all they could extract from him was the promise: "*Je prierrai pourr vous,*" with a strong trilling of dental r's, because he had an old-fashioned provincial accent. They found the answer disappointing.

The issue involves two problems, one moral the other philosophical. To the question: "Have you the right to defend by force that which you consider to be yours?", the instinctive answer is "Yes, of course!" But to the question: "Can there be absolute ownership?", the Absurdist reply must be "No". Proudhon's aphorism: "*La propriété, c'est le vol*" is a graphic expression of the fact that all ownership, if traced back far enough, is ultimately based on conquest or appropriation, later disguised to some extent by the replacement of concrete physical force by the abstract force of money or some legalistic formula. The effect of William the Conqueror's arbitrary distribution of land among his followers almost a thousand years ago is still visible in England, although considerably whittled down by democratisation and progressive taxation. Just over a hundred years before Hitler became Caesar in France, Napoleon had been Caesar in Austria, Germany and other parts of Europe; still floating in his wake is the Swedish royal family, descended from one of his marshals. And, to refer back to the Ancient World, long before the creation of the Roman Empire, the Jews, under "God's" guidance, returned to their supposed fatherland and drove out several of the tribes resident there.[27]

The paradox that the Absurdist must recognise, no doubt with regret, is that, in the last resort and in one way or another, might is right. Possession is never philosophically absolute, but it can become so strong through duration and custom as to be modifiable only by the application or the threat of force. Since absolute equality or fairness can never be more than an ideal or an aspiration, never a total reality, the existing balance of possession or ownership is always open

---

[27] In comparing God and his Son, I should perhaps have stressed more forcibly that the Lord of the Old Testament is very land-conscious and has no compunction about the use of force. He is of the world worldly, whereas Jesus is not land-conscious at all; "he hath not where to lay his head," nor does he expect that any splendid house should be built in his honour; he might well have been shocked by the concrete grandeur of the Christian cathedrals. This concrete/abstract duality of the Christian religion is no doubt a tactical strength; when a Christian nation stages a thanksgiving service after a military victory, it is addressing the Old Testament God; in the intervals of peace, it can afford to be more spiritual and to concentrate rather on Jesus. It has one foot in this world and the other, purportedly, in the Beyond.

to question. Even a politician who is genuinely trying to reduce inequality may have to call out the troops or send in the police to maintain order while he is doing so. The arm of the law, the reserve of brute force, like the poor, you have always with you, and the fundamental and ever-renewed question is: "who actually controls it? *Quis custodiet custodem?*"

It is a real problem, as well as a myth, but it is constantly complicated by the unreal imaginings of the religious myth. As is plain from the innumerable politico-religious conflicts of the past and from those raging at the moment, the vacuous and all-purpose term "God" is a virus that has been present in the linguistic system of civilisation throughout recorded history. This, I fear, is the basic lesson to be deduced from a reading of the Bible.

10

A Postscript on Paul

If Jesus was as I imagine him – that is, a God-obsessed human being with a mad nostalgia for the inaccessible Beyond, which drove him to self-sacrifice – I can understand how much he may have impressed the people who knew him when he was alive. But how they came to believe in his miracles and in those supposedly performed by the prophets and the apostles, is beyond my comprehension, because, in the course of a long life, I have never witnessed any phenomenon that ran counter to the laws of nature, as established by scientific enquiry. In my teens, however, I encountered a Salvation Army woman captain, who had a saintly aura. She did not perform miracles, but she radiated a quiet serenity which commanded respect. I wish now I had been bold enough to ask her about her relationship to Christianity. Did she believe in the dogma, or was her faith a given, inarticulate part of her make-up, unrelated to any precise theological details? If the latter were the case, this would explain why "saints" seem to occur in some, if not all, religions, whatever the institutionalised pattern of any particular faith.

One question strikes me as paramount. How can you "love" God, when he is an abstraction? What content can you give to his being? The Old Testament prophets concretise God into a Person, who demands praise and love, and tries to obtain them by inspiring fear; hence the bleak definition of the virtuous as "God-fearing." In the

Gospels, on the contrary, Jesus concretises himself as love, and tries to project this concept back onto God the Father, but with little success, it seems to me. The Old Testament God is like an ogre in a fairy-tale. As for Jesus, if he was a historical character, he may well have been awe-inspiring for those people who knew him, but for me, who did not know him, he can have no more immediate reality than any other historical figure, such as Napoleon, say, or a character, however life-like, invented by a novelist or a playwright. I cannot grasp the concept of the "living" Christ, enthroned in eternity, with whom we are supposed to have an emotional relationship. "Do you love Jesus?" is, for me, a meaningless question, for how can you feel strongly about a being of wraith-like insubstantiality? I may knock on the moonlit-door, but, as Walter de la Mare implies in his poem, "The Listeners," no-one comes to answer. Yet I have known Catholics who spoke about Jesus, the Virgin Mary and the Saints as if they were neighbours living on an upper floor, and I remember the dubious celebrations of at least one *année mariale*.

The promise of a life beyond leaves me just as unmoved; it is reminiscent of the proverbial French barber's sign: *On rasera gratis demain*. I agree that a metaphysical approach to life in inescapable for the thinking mind – man does not live by bread alone; we should see our problems against the background of the mystery of the universe, but it is presumptuous, and ultimately harmful, to encapsulate the mystery in a crude and muddled fable such as the doctrine of Redemption.

As we move to the later part of the New Testament, we find that the doctrine is repeated in a simpler and more emphatic form by a new character, who takes over from Christ. The title "The Acts of the Apostles," might lead one to suppose that, following the death of Jesus, the eleven disciples remaining after the suicide or spontaneous dissolution (cf. Acts 1. 18) of Judas Iscariot, went forth to spread the Gospel in all directions. Perhaps they did to some extent, as is suggested by the Epistle of Peter. But the man who dominates this last phase is Paul. He was not a disciple who had known Jesus, but a convert. He had his personal revelation on the road to Damascus, when Jesus, already in the Beyond, called down from above to reproach him for his initial persecution of the Christians. He is another ambiguous figure with a double identity like Moses, the Jewish Egyptian. He was a Roman citizen, ready to proclaim his status as such, and also originally an orthodox Jew. After his conversion, he was above all a self-elected apostle, more active apparently than the former disciples and, knowing, it seems, Greek as well as Hebrew, able to carry his message to Gentiles and Jews alike.

The concept of the poacher turned game-keeper is well-known. Paul is an interesting case of the game-keeper turned poacher, poaching individuals away from one set of religious beliefs – orthodox Judaism or paganism – to acceptance of his version of Christianity, which he canvasses with exceptional dogmatic fervour. He gives no explanation of his conversion; if you cannot believe, as he does, that it was a miracle, you have to fall back on the supposition of an epileptic fit, a trance or a delusion – at any rate, a thunderclap which completely reversed his action. He was as convinced of his mission as Jesus was of being the Son of God, but he saw himself not as a front-line Messiah, but as the Messiah's right-hand man, badgering orthodox Jews and unconverted Gentiles into belief, organising them into communities so that they could huddle together to keep themselves metaphysically warm and – with many protestations of love and respect – imposing on them the discipline of his will and his moral conviction, which are enunciated more sternly than Christ's. He is the first major managerial figure of the international church, more forceful, it would appear, than any of the original disciples, and the first authoritarian perhaps to use the dread disciplinary term "anathema". I have been unable to discover from the reference books around me why it was not he but Peter, who

117

became originally associated with the papal role; it is true that, for a time, Peter was bishop of Rome, but he was obviously the less commanding figure of the two.

It was certainly Paul, more definitely than Jesus, who broke away from the cramping restrictions of Jewish law by decreeing that former pagans could be welcomed into the Christian Church without submitting to the orthodox rite of circumcision. In this sense he could be called a liberator, facilitating the spread of the Christian religion. On the other hand, since he swallows the doctrine of the Redemption and the belief in the after-life hook, line and sinker, without saying anything to make them more plausible, one can deplore the fact that he was spreading dogmas, the effects of which have often been disastrous.

He remains controversial in some respects, even for Christians. I notice that he gives his own little twist to Christ's genealogy by saying that Jesus "was born of the seed of David *according to the flesh*". (Rom. 1. 2.) If the phrase has a meaning, it can only be that Joseph shared the impregnation of Mary with God – a heresy I have not seen mentioned elsewhere.

He must disappoint those who believe that religion has a relevance to politics, because he is as quietist as Jesus, or as prudent as Hobbes: –

Let every soul be in subjection to the higher powers: for there is no power but of God: and the powers that be are ordained of God. Therefore, he that resisteth the power, withstandeth the ordinance of God.

For rulers are not a terror to the good work, but to the evil. And wouldst thou have no fear of the power? do that which is good, and thou shalt have praise from the same. (Rom. 13. 1-3.)

He continued to "do good" during the reign of Nero; however, according to tradition, he did not receive "praise from the same," but martyrdom, which, one hopes, he was able to accept willingly as "God's ordinance".

Although so robustly active, he was, to some extent, a life-hater, a nay-sayer, who posited an absolute distinction between the carnal and the spiritual as the lower and the higher. In particular, he had a very grudging tolerance of the sexual instinct, as if it were a most unfortunate part of God's creation, and this attitude has blighted his particular strain of Christianity throughout the centuries. He does not seem to realise that if his personal urge to celibacy were universal, God's mysterious creative purpose, whatever it is, would come to a halt: –

It is good for a man not to touch a woman.
But, because of fornications, let each man have his own wife, and let each woman have her own husband.

But I say to the unmarried and to widows.
It is good for them to abide even as I.
But if they have not continency, let them marry, for it is better to marry than to burn. (Cor. I 7. 1-8.)

Surely, only a warped mind could coin the strange phrase: "it is better to marry than to burn".

Yet his various epistles, which are so intensely personal and, in effect, constitute a "Gospel according to St. Paul," bristling with contradictions as much as any book in the Bible, contain some of the finest rhetorical passages to be found anywhere. As I have had occasion to admit, there are biblical texts which can be moving even for the non-believer, although they have no rational sense, and perhaps no definable symbolic sense either. They are examples of what might be called the inexplicably poetic "phatic". They do not take the non-believer any nearer to conviction, but they can be enjoyed for their own sake, as mysterious verbal music. Of the many possible instances, I have already mentioned two; the second verse of Genesis I, with its wonderful, solemn rhythm: –

And the earth was without form and void: and darkness was

upon the face of the deep. And the Spirit of God moved upon the face of the waters.

and the haunting threnody of Ecclesiastes 12: –

Remember now thy Creator in the days of thy youth, while the evil days come not, nor the years draw nigh, when thou shalt say, I have no pleasure in them... etc.

A third instance, which one would hardly have expected from the rather bullying Paul, is the tender litany on charity or love, which fills chapter thirteen of Corinthians I: –

Though I speak with the tongues of men and of angels and have not love, I am become as sounding brass or a tinkling cymbal.[28]

---

[28] The passage raises some awkward problems of translation, which I confine to a note, so as not to weary the reader uninterested in technicalities.

The key word in Greek is agape, which the Authorised Version renders as "charity" and the Revised Version as "love". (A corresponding variation occurs in the French texts I have been using; the strictly Catholic Jerusalem Bible keeps to *charité*, while the more modern Bayard Version opts for *amour*). This, I think, is an instance where the Revised Version is to be preferred to the Authorised. "Love" is the warmer of the two words; there is an off-putting set phrase in English, "as cold as charity," in which the word refers to alms.

Another point: the Revised Version of the first verse "I am become sounding brass or a clanging cymbal" is inferior to the Authorised "as sounding brass or a tinkling cymbal," which makes a pleasing contrast between bombastic speech and superficiality.

The most difficult point occurs in verse 12 with the word "glass" or "mirror". The Greek term is *esoptron*, which the dictionary translates as "mirror". However, in the Ancient World, a mirror would more probably be of polished metal rather than of glass, the silvering of glass having not yet been invented. In a glass mirror, everything is clear, unless the glass is foxed; in a polished metal mirror, the reflection would probably be less distinct, hence "darkly". The Revised Version is technically correct in putting "we see in a mirror darkly," although the modern reader would not think spontaneously of a metal mirror. The Jerusalem Bible is similarly correct: "*Nous voyons à présent dans un miroir, en énigme*". But the Bayard Version is incorrect: "*Nous voyons tout pour l'instant à travers un miroir de façon énigmatique!*" Alice may have gone Through the Looking Glass into Wonderland, but no-one can see through a mirror, unless it belongs to the special modern sort, invisible on one side, which is used apparently in police interrogation-rooms, and in brothels for voyeurs. *(cont. over)*

Here, of course, love is not the sexually passionate eros of the Song of Songs, but a much broader emotion. Perhaps we have to understand it as a sort of generalised benevolence towards all mankind, a reluctance to be too presumptuous and, *mirabile dictu*, an uncertainty about dogma in face of the mystery of life: –

> For we know in part, and we prophesy in part. But when that which is perfect is come, that which is in part shall be done away.

This, like the atmosphere of Ecclesiastes, comes close to Absurdism. The Absurdist could not be more conscious of knowing only in part but, while he may have his inarticulate, secular faith to keep him going, he has no certainty that the perfect will come, either here or is some unimaginable Beyond. The arrogant verb "to prophesy" has no place in the modest vocabulary of Absurdism.

The seventeenth-century translators of the Authorised Version, deliberately or by happy accident, replaced the confusing idea of the mirror altogether by the metaphor of semi-opaque glass, more comprehensible to themselves and their readers. The meaning is: "Now we understand God (and the world) only dimly, as we see a dim reflection of our face in a metal mirror, but then we shall see God clearly face to face, as clearly as he already sees us." To get the maximum effect of the text in English, we have to combine the better points of the two different versions.

P.S. I was quite pleased with myself for working out this little puzzle of the mirror, but my son, on checking through the Internet, tells me that the issue has also been dealt with by Professor William Harris of Middlebury College, Vermont, no doubt to the same effect.

Index